n Steps to a Federal Job® or Internship for Students and Recent Grads

STUDENT'S FEDERAL CAREER GUIDE

4th Edition

Kathryn Troutman

By the Author of Best-Selling and Award-Winning Federal Job Search Books

RESUME PLACE
BUILDING CAREERS IN THE US GOVERNMENT

Resume Place, Inc.
Federal Career Publishers

1012 Edmondson Ave.
Catonsville, MD 21228
(410) 744 4324

www.resume-place.com
Email: resume@resume-place.com

Printed in the United States of America
Student's Federal Career Guide, 4th Edition: ISBN 978-1-7334076-2-5

Attention Career Counselors, Transition Counselors, Veterans' Representatives, Workforce Counselors: The Student's Federal Career Guide is a training program "handout" to support the Ten Steps to a Federal Job® workshops and PowerPoint program, which is taught at military bases, universities, one-stops, and Department of Defence agencies worldwide. To be licensed to teach the Ten Steps to a Federal Job® curriculum as a Certified Federal Job Search Trainer, go to www.resume-place.com

Book Credits
Publication Team

Developmental Editor: Paulina Chen
Cover and Interior Page Design: Brian Moore
Case Study Editors: Paulina Chen, Rita Chambers, John Gagnon, Ph.D.
Contributor: Emily Troutman and Addison J. Chen
Federal Human Resources Reviewer: Charles Clark
Illustrator: Russell Yerkes
Co-Author for the First Edition and Contributor to the Second and Third Editions:
Emily Troutman, MPP and Paul Binkley, Ph.D.

Table of Contents

Table of Contents

Federal Resume Samples

Federal Resume Samples

117-119 **Shawn** Air Force Veteran, Budget Analyst, GS-0560-9
MBA, Business and Logistics, Accounting, Managerial Finance

120-122 **Jeremy Denton** USMC Veteran, Intelligence Analyst, GS-0132-9
BA, Government and Public Policy, Legal Ethics, Governance (3 pages)

123-126 **Greg Martinez** IT Specialist (Cyber / Information Assurance), GS-22201-7
BS, Computer Science; Minors: Statistics and Economics

127-130 **Anne Crane** Health Insurance Specialist, GS-0107-9 (target GS 12)
1 year Ph.D Studies, Counseling Psychology; MS, Applied Psychology

131-134 **Phillip Sang** Mechanical Engineer, GS-0830-9 (target GS 12)
MS, Aerospace Engineering; BS, Aerospace Engineering;
BS, Mechanical Engineering

135-136 **Marisol Mendez** Army National Guard, MPP, National Security Policy
MA, Applied History; Archives and Manuscripts, Study and Writing of History

Introduction
by Kathryn Troutman

THE FEDERAL GOVERNMENT IS RECRUITING NEW GRADUATES! There is a "CLIFF" of retirements starting, and there are many openings for new graduates.

Students have great advantages when looking for a Federal job. Here are a few to consider:
- ★ The Pathways Internships offer a great way to begin a Federal career.
- ★ If you go to a career expo, it is possible that a human resources manager can hire you there directly.
- ★ You have the option to negotiate tuition reimbursement when you are hired into the Federal government.

But here is a point that many graduates miss. The Federal government is a wonderful choice for launching a career in many fields because you will gain the background that is invaluable for moving around later in any employment sector: government, corporate, non-profit, small business, academia, etc. With the experience you gain from a Federal job, you will be highly qualified to move into your next career step!

For example, if you are working in the following fields, here are some key agencies that would be an ideal launch for your career:
- ★ Finance: SEC, FDIC, CFPB
- ★ Public Health: CDC, HHS, SSA, NIH
- ★ Science: DOE, DOI
- ★ Information Technology: Any agency!
- ★ Intel: FBI, DOD, State Department
- ★ Space: NASA, US Space Command

This is the ultimate NEW GRADUATE FEDERAL JOB SEARCH RESOURCE with a clear layout of steps to get hired for a Federal job. The book is updated with the latest Federal hiring information and contains real-life Federal resume samples, which are longer than private sector two-page resumes. See the brand new information in this edition, including how to negotiate your Federal job offer.

Good luck beginning your government career!
Kathryn Troutman
President of The Resume Place, Inc., author, and publisher

Ten Steps to a Federal Job® or Internship for Students & Recent Grads

STEP 01 Accomplishments

STEP 02 Federal Student Hiring 101

STEP 03 Search for Jobs

STEP 04 Vacancy Announcements and Keywords

STEP 05 Basic Federal Resume

STEP 06 Best Federal Resume Format

STEP 07 Apply on USAJOBS

STEP 08 Interview

STEP 09 Negotiate Your Job Offer

STEP 10 Become a Permanent Federal Employee

STEP 01 Accomplishments

What is your best college, internship, or work story?
It's time to stand out above the competition!

Accomplishments

A superintendent for the National Park Service at Ellis Island and Statue of Liberty, New York, was looking for the people to interview for Seasonal Park Ranger positions, and he said, "We receive about 900 resumes. Human resources eliminates about 600 that are missing documents and the specialized experience that is required. Then, from the remaining 300, I have to find 20 to interview. What I am looking for is the SPARKLE in the resume, something that stands out and would be interesting for me to discuss in the interview, something that demonstrates the ability of the applicant to be a Summer Park Ranger here at Ellis Island."

Are you ready to get started? Accomplishments are a great first step, because everyone has accomplishment stories to tell, and these stories are critical to making your resume, questionnaire, and interviews SPARKLE.

And yet, so many jobseekers overlook this powerful tool.
If you learn this step, you will have a distinct advantage over your competition.

Writing accomplishment stories that sparkle starts with a few simple questions:
- ★ What is INTERESTING in your resume?
- ★ What have you done in your college work, internships, or positions that is IMPRESSIVE and made a difference?

Interesting and impressive accomplishments can come from:
- ★ College courses, papers, projects
- ★ Internship projects and challenges
- ★ Work experiences, challenges, and lessons learned
- ★ Travel, sports, interests, speaking, writing projects, hobbies

Think about your best accomplishments, make a list, and add these compelling stories to your resume, questionnaires, and interview answers. This is NOT bragging. You are learning to tell YOUR stories in a memorable way that will help you get interviews and get hired.

Top Five List of Accomplishments

Start brainstorming a list of your top five accomplishments from school, work, volunteering, or hobbies. What are you most proud of? What problems did you solve? Generate as many as you can think of, then narrow the list down to about five accomplishments that you will develop into accomplishment stories.

Some ideas to get you started:
★ Work experience (awards, recognition, special projects, challenges overcome)
★ Major paper or project, such as a capstone project or thesis
★ Volunteer activities
★ Clubs and other activities (athletics, debate, performing arts, music)
★ Interests (such as robotics, gaming, fitness, outdoor)

CCAR

Your accomplishments can actually be told in a memorable story-telling format called CCAR, which stands for *Context, Challenge, Action, Result*. When you write your accomplishments using the CCAR format, you can use these stories in your resume, questionnaire answers, and interview. ***They are the key to making you stand out as an applicant.***

★ ## CONTEXT

The context should include the role you played in this example. Were you a team member, planner, organizer, facilitator, administrator, or coordinator? Also, include your job title at the time and the timeline of the project. You may want to note the name of the project or situation.

★ ## CHALLENGE

What was the specific problem that you faced that needed resolution? Describe the challenge of the situation. If the challenge is difficult to write, you can try writing the challenge last.

★ ## ACTION

What did you do that made a difference? List out the specific actions you took.

★ ## RESULTS

What difference did it make? Did this new action save dollars or time? Did it increase accountability and information? Did the team achieve its goals?

Write your story with the Resume Place accomplishment tool:
https://resume-place.com/resources/ccar-accomplishment-builder/

Accomplishment Examples

Here are some real examples on how the CCAR formula helps tell a compelling, memorable story about your accomplishment for your resume, questionnaire essays, and interviews.

Independent Research Project - BS in Biology, seeking FDA position

Context: Conducted independent research to develop processes that reduce organics and chemical oxygen demand in brewery wastewater prior to discharge.

Challenge: This project was a significant investment in time as we had to build and deconstruct the project, run the research, and prepare a presentation of the findings. We also had equipment failures that needed to be fixed.

Action: Managed a research team from beginning to end. Collected water and soil samples, analyzed organic removal, and developed lab reports for peer and professor review. Investigated equipment failures and developed alternative solutions.

Result: Successfully presented research findings at the 2019 Sonoma State University's Science Symposium.

 See how this accomplishment was used in the resume:

INDEPENDENT RESEARCH PROJECT, SONOMA STATE UNIVERSITY: Managed team that conducted extensive research to develop processes to reduce organics and chemical oxygen demand in brewery wastewater prior to discharge. Routinely collected water and soil samples, analyzed organic removal, and developed lab reports for peer and professor review. Investigated equipment failures and developed alternate solutions. Presented research findings to a panel of judges at the 2019 Sonoma State University's Science Symposium.

Class Project - MBA, Supply Chain Management

Context: For my Operations Research class project, I worked with the Eagle Fitness Center to build a shift schedule.

Challenge: The student employees had a wide range of availability due to class schedules and the constraints placed by the university on the maximum number of shifts permitted by student types, creating over 400 decision variables.

Action: I set up the schedule using Microsoft Excel and Linear Programming.

Result: The process I set up successfully produced an optimized solution.

 See how this accomplishment was used in the resume:

BA 511 Operations Research   1/2019 to 4/2019

Eagle Fitness Center, Staff scheduling

Assisted the Eagle Fitness Center management in building a highly complex shift schedule. The schedule needed to place all student employees with consideration for their class schedules and availability, as well as constraints placed by the university on maximum number of shifts permitted by student type. There were over 400 decision variables, and by using Microsoft Excel and Linear Programming, I was able to produce an optimal schedule.

Summer Public Health Internship - World Health Organization
MBA in Health Administration

 See how this accomplishment was used in the resume:

Human Resources Management Intern   6/2011 to 8/2011

The World Health Organization
Avenue Appia 20 Geneva, Switzerland 1211

WHO PERFORMANCE MANAGEMENT AND DEVELOPMENT SYSTEM: Assisted in the planning and implementation of a strengthened Performance Management and Development System (PMDS) across the Organization. This included preparations of a Pilot Programme to test an improved version of the PMDS (Performance Management), liaising and coordinating with 5 participating regional offices, generation of support documentation, data collection, data analysis and formatting to monitor progress of the Pilot and evaluating the impact of the improved PMDS. The Pilot project comprised of 800 participants from all the WHO Regional Offices. This is the first Pilot undertaken by HR of its sort in the UN system.

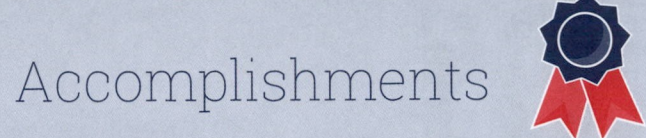

You may end up adding very short accomplishments to your resume in a way that adds great impact. Look at what a difference accomplishments makes in this sample Education block from a resume:

 Dull Education section:

California State Polytechnic University, Pomona, CA   (09/2016-06/2018)
College of Business, Bachelor of Science, Computer Information Systems   GPA: 3.80

 Exciting Education section:

California State Polytechnic University, Pomona, CA   (09/2016-06/2018)
College of Business, Bachelor of Science, Computer Information Systems   GPA: 3.80

- Graduated with Magna Cum Laude honors distinction, June 2018
- CyberCorps: Scholarship-for-Service Program, September 2017-June 2018
- Dean's List, September 2016-June 2018
- President's List, California State Polytechnic University, Pomona, May 2017

Relevant coursework: Systems Development Project, **Digital Forensics**, Network Security, **Information Systems Auditing, Internet Security,** Intermediate Java Programming, Management Information Systems, Interactive and Responsive Web Development, Database Design and Development, Systems Analysis and Design, and Business Telecommunications

ACADEMIC PROJECTS - BS, Computer Information Systems

DATA ANALYTICS PROJECT MANAGER (03/2018-05/2018): To help shape the planning and organizing of the Social Innovation Lab at Cal Poly Pomona, distributed a campus-wide survey to over 23,717 students to assess lab user needs. Analyzed the survey data of over 300 students.

Practice Writing the CCAR Format

Let's practice putting your accomplishment stories into the CCAR formula. Remember to keep it straightforward. We like to think of the CCAR formula as something that makes writing easier, rather than harder. The goal is to end up with about 3 to 7 sentences for each accomplishment story. The Federal Human Resources Specialists and Managers want to see MORE details about your accomplishments than private sector managers.

★ **CONTEXT**

★ **CHALLENGE**

★ **ACTION**

★ **RESULTS**

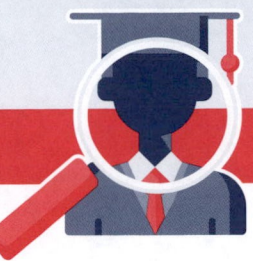

STEP 02 Federal Student Hiring 101

Understanding Federal hiring, Pathways, and internship programs can help you break into government

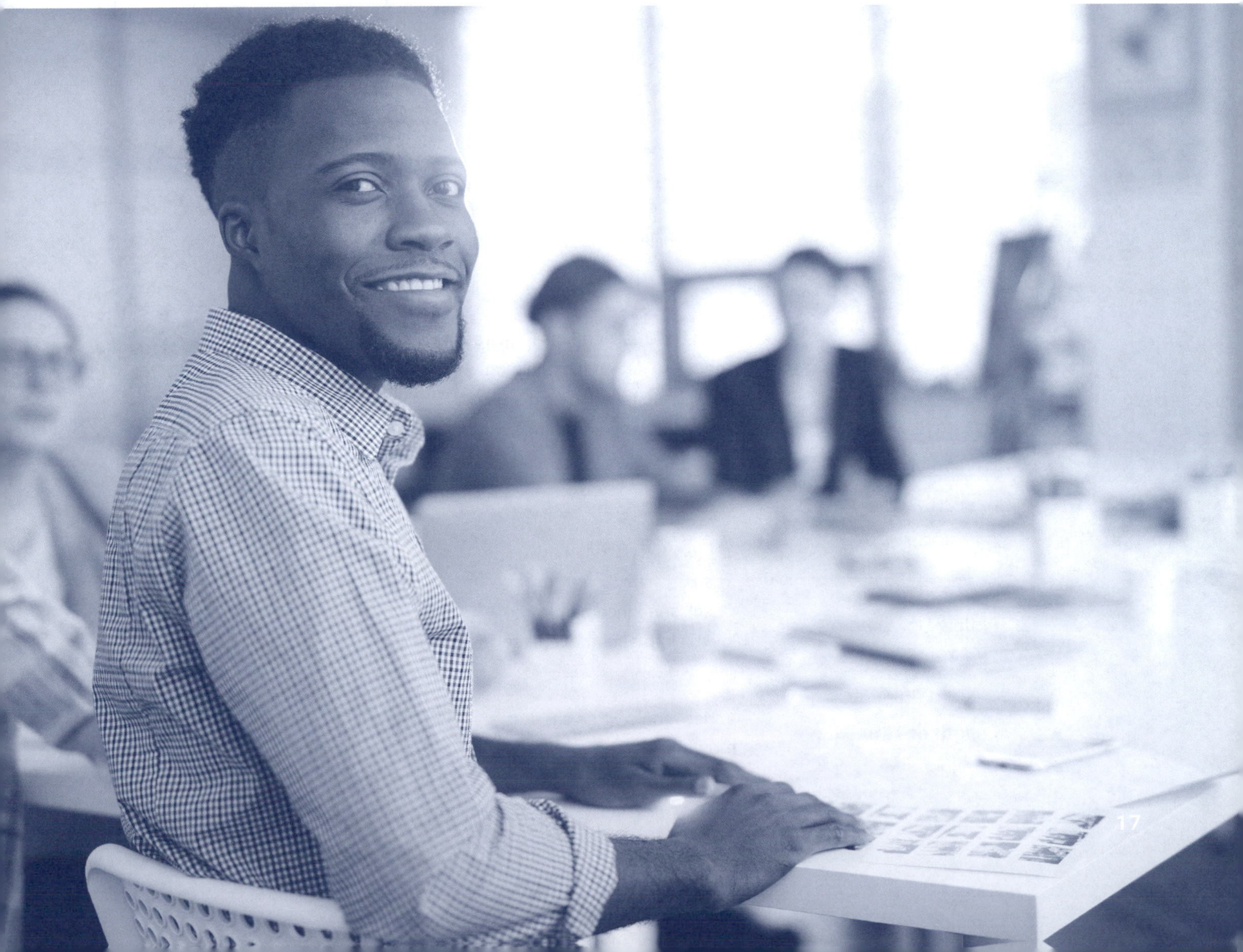

How Is Finding a Federal Job Different from Private Industry?

The general process is basically the same between applying for a private sector and a Federal job, but there are some differences to be aware of before you start a Federal job search.

Key differences between a private sector and Federal job search

	Private Sector Job Search	Federal Job Search
Student Resume Length	1 to 2 pages	2 to 4 pages
Cover Letter	Required or highly recommended	Not required or recommended for application. Use if networking.
Transcripts	Send if needed	Required
Job Search	Look on job websites	Look for jobs on USAJOBS or agency websites
How to Apply	Send cover letter and resume or apply online	Apply online at USAJOBS or agency websites
Qualifications	Read the Qualifications Required section to determine minimum qualifications (education and experience) required for the position	Read the Specialized Experience section of the announcement. You must meet the stated minimum qualifications to be considered for the position. Meet additional qualifications in order to get Best Qualified. 
Interviews	Variety of formats	The Federal interview is a TEST, usually Behavioral-Based open-ended questions.
Follow Up	Check announcement for follow-up info or contact person	Track your applications in USAJOBS; check announcement for HR contact for additional questions
Length of Time	Varies (could be as short as a month)	Generally longer than private sector; Office of Personnel Management states 80 days from the announcement closing to the job offer.

Overview

Students and recent graduates do have many opportunities to work for the Federal government.

First, anyone who is qualified to compete for a Federal job can apply, regardless of whether or not you are a student.

In addition, the Federal government also offers the Pathways program, which provides three additional types of programs specifically for current students and recent graduates (see pages xx).

For current students, other student opportunities are also mentioned on page xx.

The hiring process is essentially the same for Federal job opportunities, whether they are part of the Pathways program or not, so the concepts taught in this book will help you apply for Pathways opportunities as well as the Federal job listings that are open to all.

Stage	Federal Job Openings	Pathways: Internships	Pathways: Recent Grads	Pathways: Presidential Management Fellows Program
During high school		✔		
During undergraduate studies	✔	✔		
Within 2 years after college	✔	✔	✔	
During graduate school	✔	✔	✔	✔ (if graduating by Aug 31 of year after application)
Within 2 years after graduate school	✔	✔	✔	✔

Pathways Program

The Pathways Program is designed to recruit young, talented people (like you!) and to develop them into the nation's next generation of world-class leaders and public servants.

This program offers you the chance to build a solid history of professional experience, "test drive" the federal government, build your federal network, and serve the public.

The Pathways Program provides three types of opportunities for students and recent graduates:

★ **Internships:** Paid opportunities to explore Federal careers for high school to graduate school and professional academic levels.

★ **Recent Grads:** Offers career development with training and mentorship for recent graduates of trade and vocational schools, community colleges, universities, and other qualifying educational institutions or programs. To be eligible, applicants must apply within two years of degree or certificate completion.

★ **Presidential Management Fellows Program:** A leadership development program for those who have completed an advanced degree within the last two years or will complete by Aug 31 of the year following application.

Key Points to Remember

1. **Know your interests:** Target agencies that interest you the most and network with people in those agencies. Many of the internships will relate to your college major.

2. **Proactively search for opportunities:** The most difficult part is simply finding these positions. Your first step should be to look on www.usajobs.gov; your second step to review specific agency websites; and your third step to review third party sites, such as that of Partnership for Public Service to see what offerings are available for students or recent graduates.

3. **It's never too early to start:** Federal hiring opportunities aimed at students often have application deadlines many months in advance of the start date. Some may require security clearances, which can take anywhere from four months to one year or more to perform. Others may have very short deadlines that pop up at inopportune times. You should start your research process early to allow time to find opportunities and to be prepared for those positions that suddenly appear.

You can learn more about these programs at www.usajobs.gov/StudentsandGrads or by clicking "Students and Recent Graduates" under the USAJOBS Resource Center menu at www.USAJOBS. gov. *www.usajobs.gov/StudentsandGrads*

Students & recent graduates

If you're a current student or recent graduate, you may be eligible for federal internships and job opportunities through the Pathways and other student programs.

Internship Program

Pathways offers students from high school through college and graduate school opportunities to gain valuable Federal experience while still in school.

Eligibility
★ You must be a current student ("student" is an all-encompassing term that includes attendees of 4-year universities, community colleges, professional and vocational schools, graduate programs, and others). Be sure to review federal requirements for eligibility as a "current student." If you are enrolled in an academic program leading to a degree or professional certification, it is likely that you qualify.

Internship Details
★ You can be hired temporarily for up to one year, or for an indefinite period pending completion of certain educational requirements.
★ You may be hired in either a full-time or part-time capacity.
★ You will sign a Participant Agreement with the agency detailing the expectations for the internship.
★ Your internship will be related to your career goals OR current field of study.

Where to Search
★ USAJOBS.gov
★ Individual agency websites

> Internships are flexible for hours, telework, and your courses/exams.

Recent Graduates Program

This program targets those who are about to graduate and those who recently graduated for developmental program positions in the Federal government. These are full-time employment positions after graduation designed to help agencies recruit, train, and retain highly qualified individuals who may not have enough experience to succeed in competitive hiring.

Eligibility

★ You must apply within 2 years of completing a degree or certificate. NOTE: if you are a veteran, in certain circumstances you can apply within 6 years.

Program Details

★ The program is designed to be dynamic and developmental in its focus, with a specific goal of preparing you for a Federal career. The program lasts for one year (unless the training requirements of the position warrant a lengthier training period).

★ As part of the developmental focus of this program, you will receive mentorship, an individual development plan, 40-hours of formal training, and career advancement opportunities.

★ You will sign a Participant Agreement with the agency.

Where to Search

★ USAJOBS.gov

★ Individual agency websites

Presidential Management Fellows (PMF)

For more than three decades, the PMF Program has been the Federal government's premier leadership development program for advanced degree candidates. The Program focuses on developing a cadre of potential government leaders.

The PMF is designed to recruit and place highly-qualified advanced-degree holders into developmental opportunities for potential permanent conversion. Successful completion of the PMF is often a fast track to the upper levels of government, including the Senior Executive Service. During their 2-year fellowship, PMFs receive rotational assignments and training opportunities intended to broaden their public leadership and management abilities.

Eligibility

★ If you will meet all advanced degree requirements (even though you have not necessarily graduated), including the completion or successful defense of any required thesis or dissertation, you are eligible to apply. Eligibility is based on completion of degree requirements by August 31st of the year following the annual application.
  – OR –

★ If you have completed an advanced degree from a qualifying college or university during the previous 2 years from the opening date of the PMF Program's annual application announcement, you are eligible to apply.

★ Advanced Degree means a professional or graduate degree (e.g., master's, Ph.D., J.D.).

Program Details

★ Fellowships are full-time paid positions with benefits and last 2 years.

★ The PMF Program includes 2 years of developmental training and performance experience in the federal government.

★ You will receive a personal mentor, be placed in occupational and functional positions, and be offered 80+ hours of annual formal training.

★ You will be placed on a performance plan during your fellowship and must be rated as "successful" for each rating period to be able to continue in the program.

★ You can see the list for each year of Finalists and the colleges from which they have graduated: *https://apply.pmf.gov/finalists.aspx*

Where to Search

Visit *www.pmf.gov*, which is the government's one-stop-shop for resources for current and potential Presidential Management Fellows. The PMF announcement is usually posted the first 2 weeks in October of each year. You can also set up a SEARCH in your USAJOBS account for Presidential Management Fellows. The announcement will be sent to you automatically. This page will even list the names of the people who are selected for PMF each year!

STUDENT'S **FEDERAL CAREER GUIDE**

Interesting Opportunities in Government for Students

Check out these popular Federal agencies and internship programs that could match your interest and college major:

 ## NASA

#BeAnAstronaut: NASA Seeks Applicants to Explore Moon, Mars: Become an Artemis Generation Astronaut

Website: *https://www.nasa.gov/astronauts*

 ## Space Force

The National Defense Authorization Act for Fiscal Year 2020 approved a new, independent Space Force within the Department of the Air Force. As this new military branch takes shape in 2020, we'll be recruiting the brightest minds in science, technology, aerospace and engineering to meet its needs.

Website: *https://www.spaceforce.mil/*
Careers: *https://www.airforce.com/careers/browse-careers/space*

★ Centers for Disease Control and Prevention (CDC)

Interested in learning more about public health science or developing leadership and critical thinking skills to provide rapid, strategic, and effective solutions to protect the public's health? We have a variety of hands-on training programs for students and recent graduates. All offer a unique experience in one of the many exciting public health fields.

★ U.S. Food and Drug Administration (FDA)

The Food and Drug Administration's (FDA) mission is to protect and advance public health by helping to speed innovations that provide our nation with safe and effective medical products and that keep our food safe and reduce harm from all regulated tobacco products. FDA employs scientists in a wide variety of fields and disciplines, including biologists, chemists, epidemiologists, nurses, pharmacists, pharmacologists, physicians, social or behavioral scientists, statisticians, veterinarians, engineers, and others.

FDA Scientific Careers:
https://www.fda.gov/about-fda/jobs-and-training-fda/scientific-careers-fda

Scientific Internships, Fellowships / Trainees and Non-U.S. Citizens:
https://www.fda.gov/about-fda/jobs-and-training-fda/scientific-internships-fellowships-

★ The Department of Homeland Security

The Department of Homeland Security offers a variety of prestigious scholarships, fellowships, internships and training opportunities to expose talented students to the broad national security mission.

Careers: *https://www.dhs.gov/homeland-security-careers/students*

The Cybersecurity Internship Program is designed to give current students an opportunity to work alongside cyber leaders with the U.S. Department of Homeland Security. Interns will have the opportunity to apply concepts, protocols, and tools acquired through coursework in the real world by working side by side with experts in cybersecurity.

Careers: *https://www.dhs.gov/homeland-security-careers/cybersecurity-internship-program-0*

★ National Security Agency

NSA offers a wide variety of programs for students in high school up through doctoral candidates.

Students: *https://www.intelligencecareers.gov/NSA/nsastudentsportal.html*

★ Federal Bureau of Investigation (FBI)

Opportunities for students on a mission.
Join an elite group of students from around the nation in one of the FBI's many programs for students and recent graduates.

Students: *https://www.fbijobs.gov/students*
Careers: *https://www.fbijobs.gov/career-paths/special-agents*

★ U.S. Environmental Protection Agency

Ever thought about having a great career dedicated to:

- ★ improving the health and well-being of all Americans?
- ★ ensuring that we have clean air, pure water, and better-protected land?

Internships, fellowships, and other opportunities are available at our Washington D.C. headquarters, in our 10 regional offices, and at our labs and research centers throughout the nation.

Internships: *https://www.epa.gov/careers/student-internships*

★ U.S. Secret Service

The Secret Service Student Volunteer Service Program is designed to provide students with an understanding of the nature and the structure of the U.S. Secret Service. The program provides unpaid, academic-related work assignments that allow students to explore career options while developing personal and professional skills.

Students: *https://www.secretservice.gov/join/diversity/students/*
Careers: *https://www.secretservice.gov/join/careers/*

★ Army Cyber Institute at West Point

The ACI Summer Internship Program (SIP)
The Summer Internship Program is an 8-week course designed to provide interns with real world experience in futuristic cyber research at it relates to the security of the nation. The interns will be exposed to the entire research cycle, from idea development to briefing a product, and how each piece of a research project integrates with a larger effort.

Careers: *https://cyber.army.mil/Engage/Work-With-Us/*

★ Department of Defense (DOD) Civilian Careers

DOD offers high-quality programs for students, graduates, and professionals.
Join an elite group of students from around the nation in one of DOD's many programs for students and recent graduates.

Internships: *https://godefense.cpms.osd.mil/internships.aspx*
Students: *https://godefense.cpms.osd.mil/student_opportunities.aspx*

Department of Defense STEM Internships allow high school and college students the opportunity to engage in hands-on research, solving real-world problems at DOD laboratories and facilities. Attend the Advanced Course in Cyber Security Bootcamp (ACE).

Internships: *https://dodstem.us/stem-programs/internships*

★ U.S. Department of Veterans Affairs

Pathways Internship Program
The Pathways Internship Program allows students to join VA in career positions that emphasize long-term training and development. As of March 2015, there are 407 current VA Recent Graduates, and 636 current VA Pathways Interns.

Internships: *https://www.vacareers.va.gov/Careers/StudentsTrainees*

STUDENT'S FEDERAL CAREER GUIDE

27

★ U.S. Department of State

There are many student programs available at the U.S. Department of State, offering you a chance to support and gain insight into U.S. foreign policy and diplomacy, explore new career avenues, and acquire lifelong skills, as you represent America to the world.

Students: *https://careers.state.gov/intern/student-programs/*

Virtual Student Federal Service (VSFS) Program—Students can work on projects that include helping counter violent extremism, strengthening human rights monitoring, developing virtual programs, engaging in digital communications, mapping, economic and political reporting, data analysis, graphic design, and app building.

★ Smithsonian

Hundreds of graduate students and holders of doctorates come to the Smithsonian to do independent research under the guidance of a member of our world-class research staff. Fellows have the opportunity to study and work intensively with Smithsonian collections and experts in their fields and beyond. In addition, more than 1,500 students pursue internships offered across the organization.

Students: *https://www.si.edu/ofi*

★ U.S. Fish and Wildlife Service

The U.S. Fish and Wildlife Service offers a large variety of internship opportunities for enrolled high school and college students, as well as recent college graduates. An internship is a great way to get to know our agency and pursue full-time employment opportunities.

Internships: *https://www.fws.gov/southeast/work-with-us/internships/*

★ National Geospatial-Intelligence Agency

NGA is pleased to announce that external applicants now have the ability to view and apply for jobs directly on the Intelligence Careers website. Visit our new website to find a student program that meets your needs, browse career fields, and view sample jobs.

Careers: *https://www.nga.mil/Careers/Pages/default.aspx*

★ National Park Service

National Park Service internships are a way to acquire hands-on work experience while helping preserve and protect the nation's natural and cultural heritage. We also recommend that you contact a park of interest directly to ensure that you know all the opportunities available.

Students: *https://www.nps.gov/subjects/youthprograms/jobs-and-internships.htm*

★ Bureau of Land Management (BLM)

The BLM offers internships that help to support American families and build strong economies while keeping public lands healthy and productive. Working individually or as part of a team or crew, BLM interns participate in the shared stewardship of public lands - building trails and enhancing recreational facilities, restoring habitat damaged by wildland fire, and supporting BLM's multiple-use mission.

Internships: *https://www.blm.gov/get-involved/internships*

The Department of the Interior Direct Hiring Authority for Resource Assistant Internship (DHA-RAI) Program is a direct hiring initiative that challenges the BLM to develop an 11-week rigorous summer internship program for current college students or recent graduates, with particular attention to African American, Asian, Pacific Islander, Native American, and Hispanic students.

Students and Grads: *https://www.blm.gov/careers/students-and-grads/direct-hire-program*

Even More Student and Recent Graduate Opportunities

★ **Air Force Civilian Careers - Internships**
https://www.afciviliancareers.com/students-and-graduates/

★ **Department of Commerce - Internships**
https://www.commerce.gov/work-with-us/internships

★ **Department of Health and Human Services - Student Jobs**
https://www.hhs.gov/careers/

★ **Health Resources and Services Administration**
https://www.hrsa.gov/hr/intern-program.html

★ **NASA - Careers**
https://www.nasa.gov/careers

★ **National Oceanic and Atmospheric Administration - Internships**
https://www.noaa.gov/work-with-us

★ **Office of Personnel Management - Presidential Management Fellowships**
www.opm.gov/pmf

★ **Social Security Administration (SSA)**
https://www.ssa.gov/careers/student1.htm

★ **United States Agency for International Development (USAID)**
https://www.usaid.gov/work-usaid/careers/student-internships

★ **US Army Cyber Command Internships**
https://www.arcyber.army.mil/

How to Find Your Grade Level

SALARY TABLE 2020-GS (Effective Jan 2020)

Grade	Step 1	Step 2	Step 3	Step 10	WGI*	Educational Qualifications for Certain Positions
1	19543	20198	20848	24448	VARIES	No education requirement
2	21974	22497	23225	27653	VARIES	High school graduation or equivalent (e.g., GED)
3	23976	24775	25574	31167	799	One year above high school
4	26915	27812	28709	34988	897	Two years above high school (or Associate's Degree)
5	30113	31117	32121	39149	1004	Four years above high school leading to a Bachelor's Degree
6	33567	34686	35805	43638	1119	
7	37301	38544	39787	48488	1243	One full year of graduate study or Bachelor's degree with Superior Academic Achievement (SAA)
8	41310	42687	44064	53703	1377	
9	45627	47148	48669	59316	1521	Master's Degree or equivalent (e.g., J.D. or LL.B.) or two years of graduate education
10	50246	51921	53596	65321	1675	
11	55204	57044	58884	71764	1840	Ph.D. or three years of graduate school, For research positions only: completion of all requirements for Master's Degree
12	66167	68373	70579	86021	2206	For research positions only: completion of all requirements for a doctoral or equivalent degree
13	78681	81304	83927	102288	2623	
14	92977	96076	99175	120868	3099	All positions at or above GS-13 require appropriate specialized experience, and do not allow education to be substituted for that specialized experience.
15	109366	113012	116658	142180	3646	

*WGI Within Grade Increases - The salary increases from Step 1 to 10.
See the full pay scale tables and locality increases at
https://www.opm.gov/policy-data-oversight/pay-leave/salaries-wages/2020/general-schedule/

STUDENT'S FEDERAL CAREER GUIDE

Superior Academic Achievement (SAA) to qualify for a GS-07 with a Bachelor's degree

Class Standing	You are in the upper third of your graduating class in your college, university, or major subdivision, such as the School of Business.
Grade Point Average (credited whichever way is more beneficial to the applicant)	a. You have a 3.0 out of a possible 4.0 ("B" or better) recorded on your transcript, or as computed based on 4 years of education, or as computed based on all courses completed during the final 2 years of your curriculum, or b. You have 3.5 or higher out of a possible 4.0 ("B+" or better) based on the average of the required courses completed in the major field or the required courses in the major field completed during the final 2 years of the curriculum.
Election to Membership in a National Honor Society	Honor societies listed in the Association of College Honor Society of American College Fraternities (1991) meet this requirement. Membership in a freshman honor society does not meet this requirement.

Useful Links

For descriptions of Federal job titles, check out the Position Classification Standards from the Office of Personnel Management. These descriptions are also a valuable source for keywords for your Federal resume.

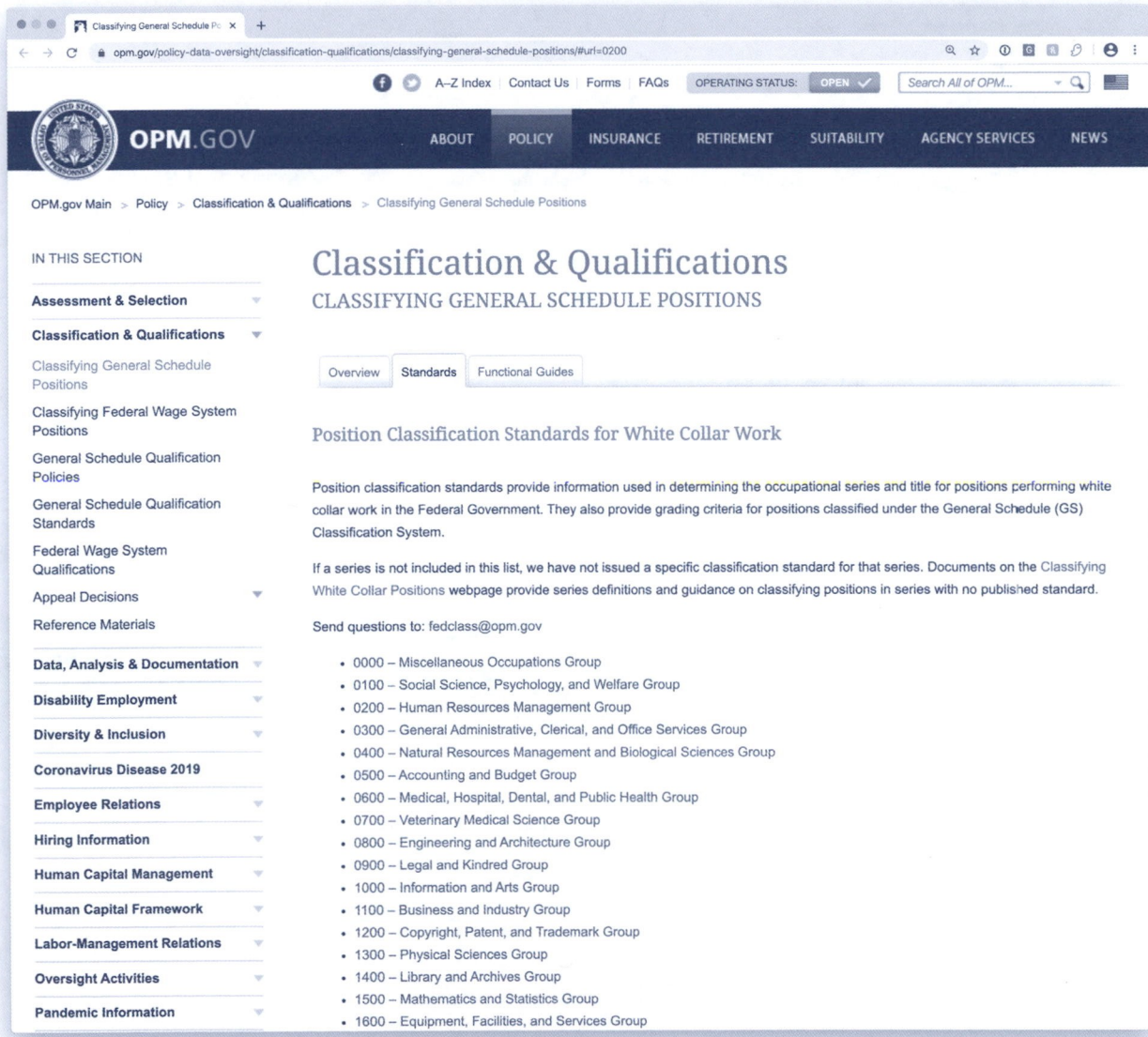

https://www.opm.gov/policy-data-oversight/classification-qualifications/classifying-general-schedule-positions/#url=0200

Useful Links

Here are some of our favorite websites to check out for your job search.

https://www.usa.gov/federal-agencies

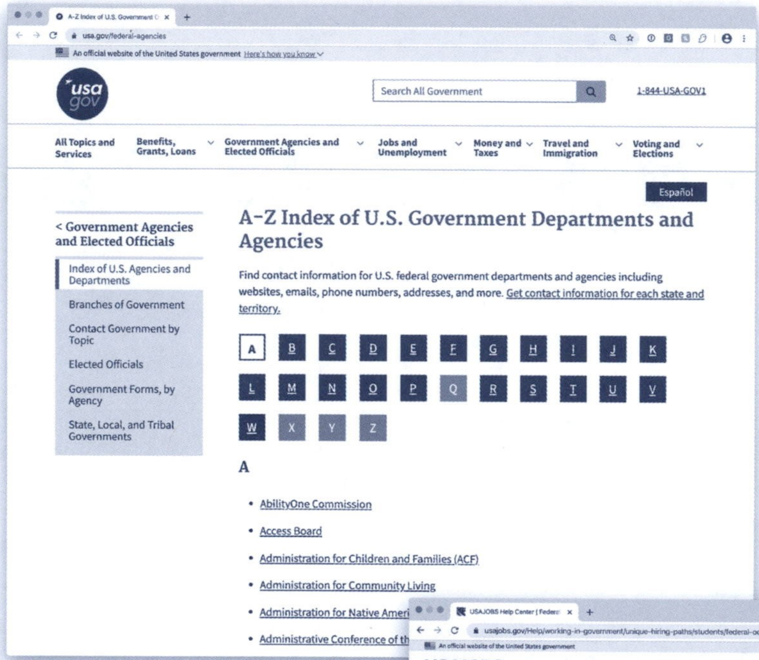

A-Z Index of U.S. Government Departments and Agencies

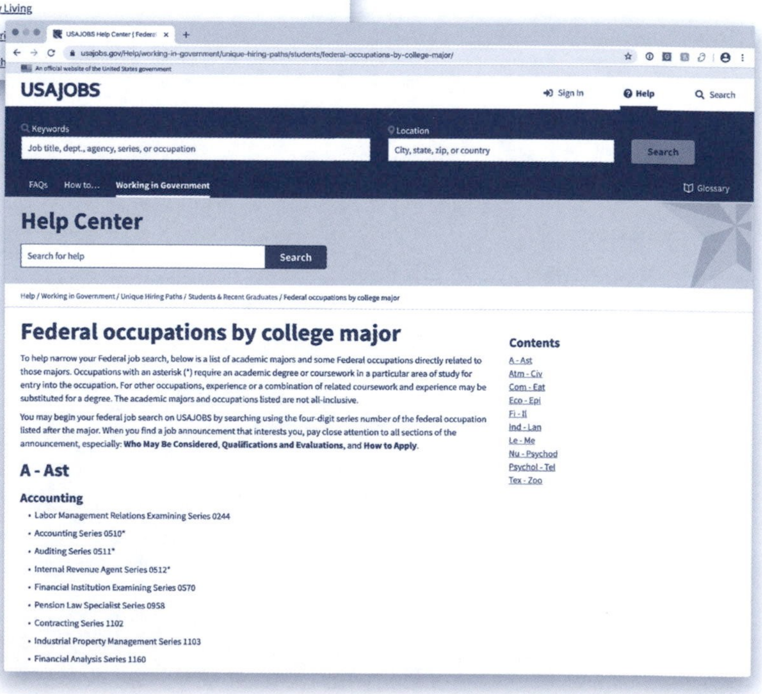

Federal Occupations by College Major - USAJOBS

https://www.usajobs.gov/Help/working-in-government/unique-hiring-paths/students/federal-occupations-by-college-major/

https://bestplacestowork.org/

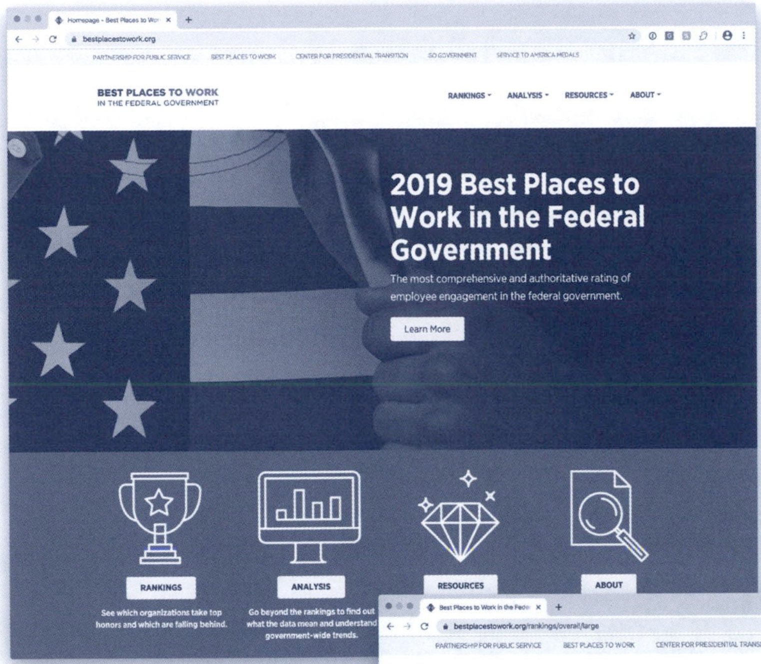

Best Places to Work in the Federal Government

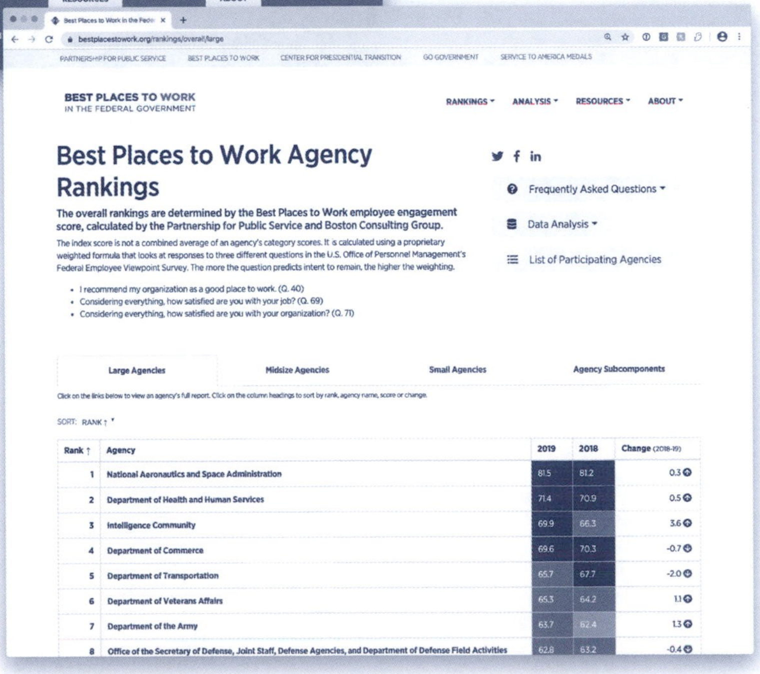

Best Places to Work Agency Rankings

https://bestplacestowork.org/rankings/overall/large

STEP 02

Useful Links

https://www.opm.gov/policy-data-oversight/disability-employment/
selective-placement-program-coordinator-directory/

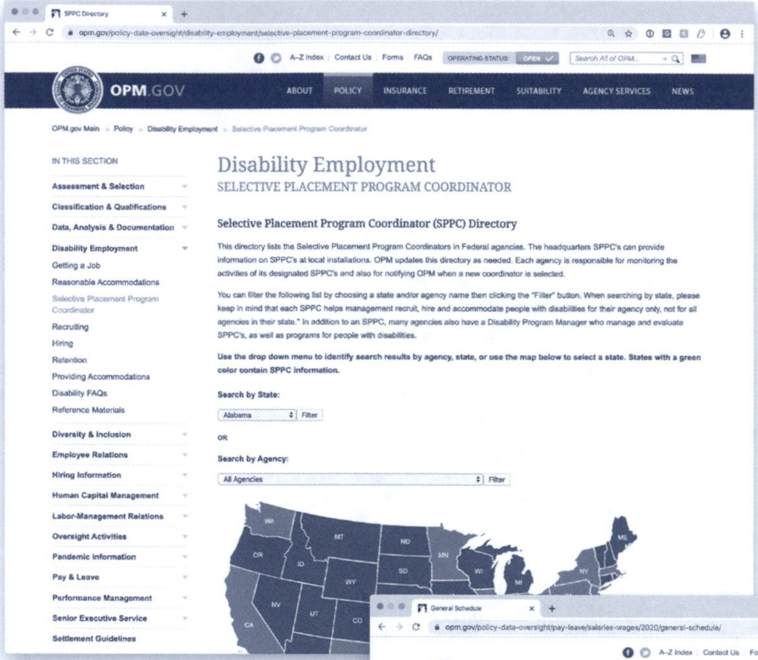

Schedule A Selective Placement Coordinators - for Federal Jobs for People with Disabilities

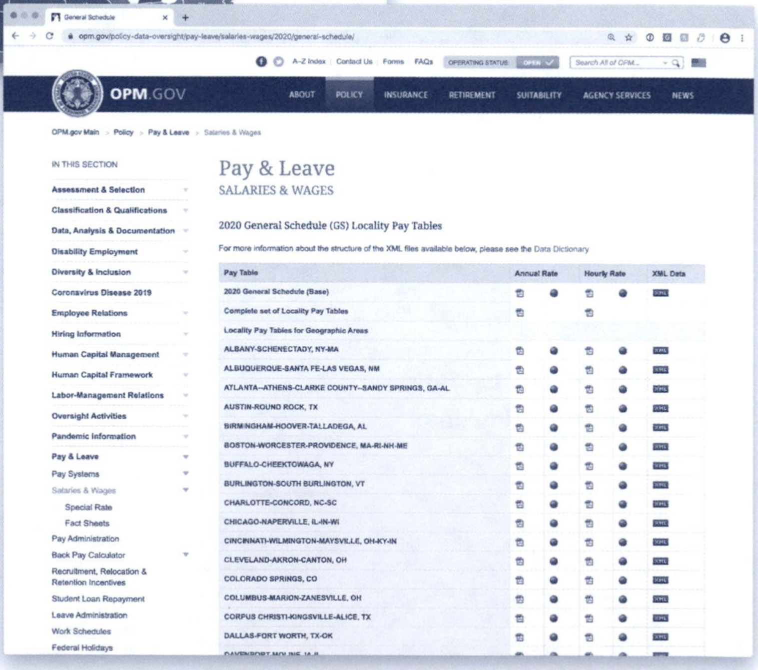

Government Salaries

https://www.opm.gov/policy-data-oversight/pay-leave/
salaries-wages/2020/general-schedule/

Student Veterans

Student Veterans' Preference

1. Veterans' preference will apply for **PUBLIC** vacancy announcements on **USAJOBS.**

How is Veterans' Preference different?

Non-disabled Veterans—If the resume is Qualified, the resume will rise to the top of the appropriate category based on your score!

Disabled Veterans—If the resume is scored and rated Qualified (**at least a score of 80**), the resume will rise to the top of the highest category, Best Qualified!

Best-Qualified
(95-100)

Well-Qualified
(90-94.9)

Qualified
(80-89.9)

Applications are reviewed, scored, and placed in one of three categories with **CATEGORY RATING**: Qualified, Well-Qualified, or Best-Qualified.

2. Active Duty service members can apply to Competitive announcements; because of the **VOW Act, veterans' preference will apply.**

Results: The veteran applications will be **reviewed EQUALLY with all other applicants.**

For more information, visit www.fedshirevets.gov or locate your Veteran Employment Program Officer at *https://www.fedshirevets.gov/veterans-council/agency-directory/*

When Veterans' Preference Does Not Apply

Although veterans' preference requires hiring officials to select qualified veterans ahead of non-veterans on announcements open to the public (up to GS-15), there is an exception for a group of positions the Office of Personnel Management identifies as Scientific and Professional Series positions. For these positions, veterans' preference only applies when filling positions at GS-9 or below. Please see below for a list of these positions:

GS-020 Community Planning
GS-101 Social Science
GS-110 Economist
GS-130 Foreign Affairs
GS-131 International Relations
GS-140 Workforce Research and
       Analysis
GS-150 Geography
GS-170 History
GS-180 Psychology
GS-184 Sociology
GS-185 Social Work
GS-190 General Anthropology
GS-193 Archeology
GS-401 General Biological Science
GS-403 Microbiology
GS-405 Pharmacology
GS-408 Ecology
GS-410 Zoology
GS-413 Physiology
GS-414 Entomology
GS-415 Toxicology
GS-430 Botany
GS-434 Plant Pathology
GS-435 Plant Physiology
GS-436 Plant Protection and
       Quarantine
GS-437 Horticulture
GS-440 Genetics
GS-454 Rangeland Management
GS-457 Soil Conservation
GS-460 Forestry
GS-470 Soil Science
GS-471 Agronomy
GS-480 General Fish and Wildlife
       Administration
GS-482 Fishery Biology
GS-485 Wildlife Refuge
       Management
GS-486 Wildlife Biology
GS-487 Animal Science
GS-510 Accounting
GS-511 Auditing
GS-512 Internal Revenue Agent

GS-601 General Health Science
GS-630 Dietitian and Nutritionist
GS-631 Occupational Therapist
GS-633 Physical Therapist
GS-635 Corrective Therapist
GS-637 Manual Arts Therapist
GS-638 Recreation/Creative Arts
       Therapist
GS-639 Educational Therapist
GS-644 Medical Technologist
GS-665 Speech Pathology and
       Audiology
GS-690 Industrial Hygiene
GS-696 Consumer Safety
GS-801 General Engineering
GS-803 Safety Engineering
GS-804 Fire Protection Engineering
GS-806 Materials Engineering
GS-807 Landscape Architecture
GS-808 Architecture
GS-810 Civil Engineering
GS-819 Environmental Engineering
GS-830 Mechanical Engineering
GS-840 Nuclear Engineering
GS-850 Electrical Engineering
GS-854 Computer Engineering
GS-855 Electronics Engineering
GS-858 Biomedical Engineering
GS-861 Aerospace Engineering
GS-871 Naval Architecture
GS-880 Mining Engineering
GS-881 Petroleum Engineering
GS-890 Agricultural Engineering
GS-892 Ceramic Engineering
GS-893 Chemical Engineering
GS-894 Welding Engineering
GS-896 Industrial Engineering
GS-1015 Museum Curator
GS-1221 Patent Adviser
GS-1223 Patent Classifying
GS-1224 Patent Examining
GS-1226 Design Patent Examining
GS-1301 General Physical Science
GS-1306 Health Physics

GS-1310 Physics
GS-1313 Geophysics
GS-1315 Hydrology
GS-1320 Chemistry
GS-1321 Metallurgy
GS-1330 Astronomy and Space
        Science
GS-1340 Meteorology
GS-1350 Geology
GS-1360 Oceanography
GS-1370 Cartography
GS-1372 Geodesy
GS-1373 Land Surveying
GS-1380 Forest Products
        Technology
GS-1382 Food Technology
GS-1384 Textile Technology
GS-1386 Photographic Technology
GS-1420 Archivist
GS-1510 Actuary
GS-1515 Operations Research
GS-1520 Mathematics
GS-1529 Mathematical Statistician
GS-1530 Statistician
GS-1550 Computer Science
GS-1701 General Education and
        Training
GS-1710 Education and Vocational
        Training
GS-1720 Education Program
GS-1725 Public Health Educator
GS-1730 Education Research
GS-1740 Education Services
GS-1750 Instructional Systems

03 Search for Jobs

Top places to look for Federal jobs and internships: USAJOBS.gov, excepted service agency websites, and job fairs

Keywords

PATHWAYS

ewing 1 – 25 of 160 jobs

🏴 Save this search. We'll email you new jobs as they become available.

Pathways, Student Trainee (Biological Sciences), ZT-0499-2 (PA

National Oceanic and Atmospheric Administration

Department of Commerce

📍 Ann Arbor, Michigan

🕐 *Open 04/24/2020 to 05/07/2020*

Pathways Recent Graduate - Public Notice Flyer Only

Centers for Medicare & Medicaid Services

How to Search USAJOBS

Here is what we recommend that you do when you start searching for internships and jobs in USAJOBS.

Search for all PATHWAYS positions on USAJOBS.

Search for Pathways positions in a certain geographic location.

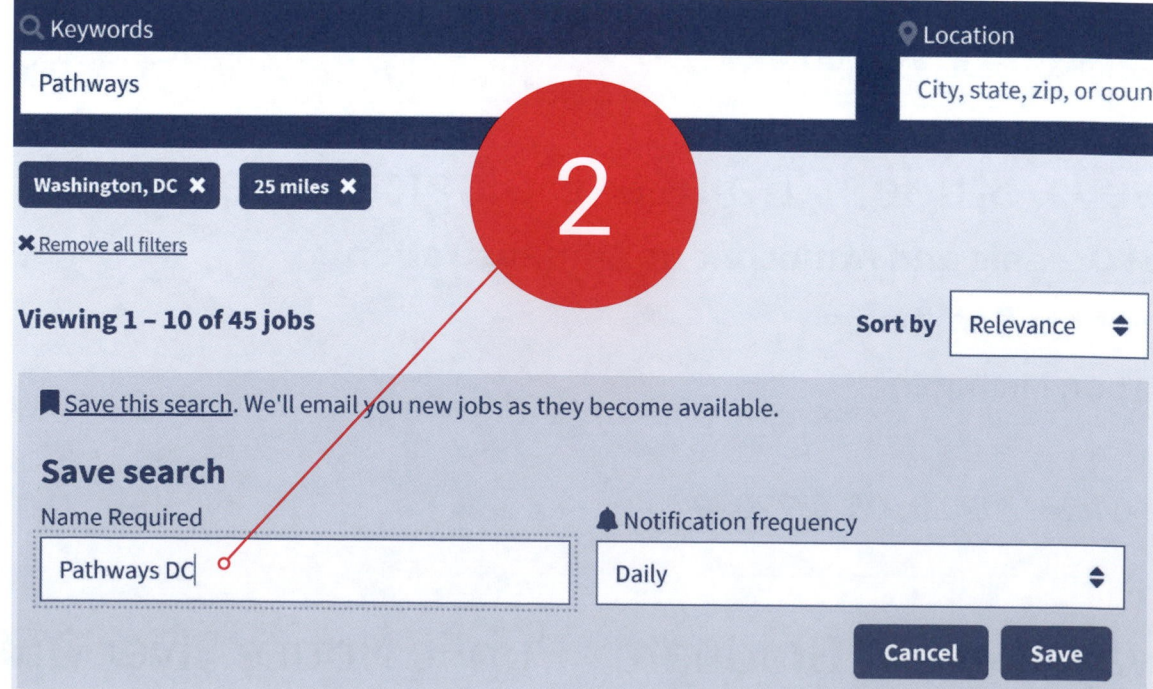

Save your searches, so that you can receive job announcements daily.

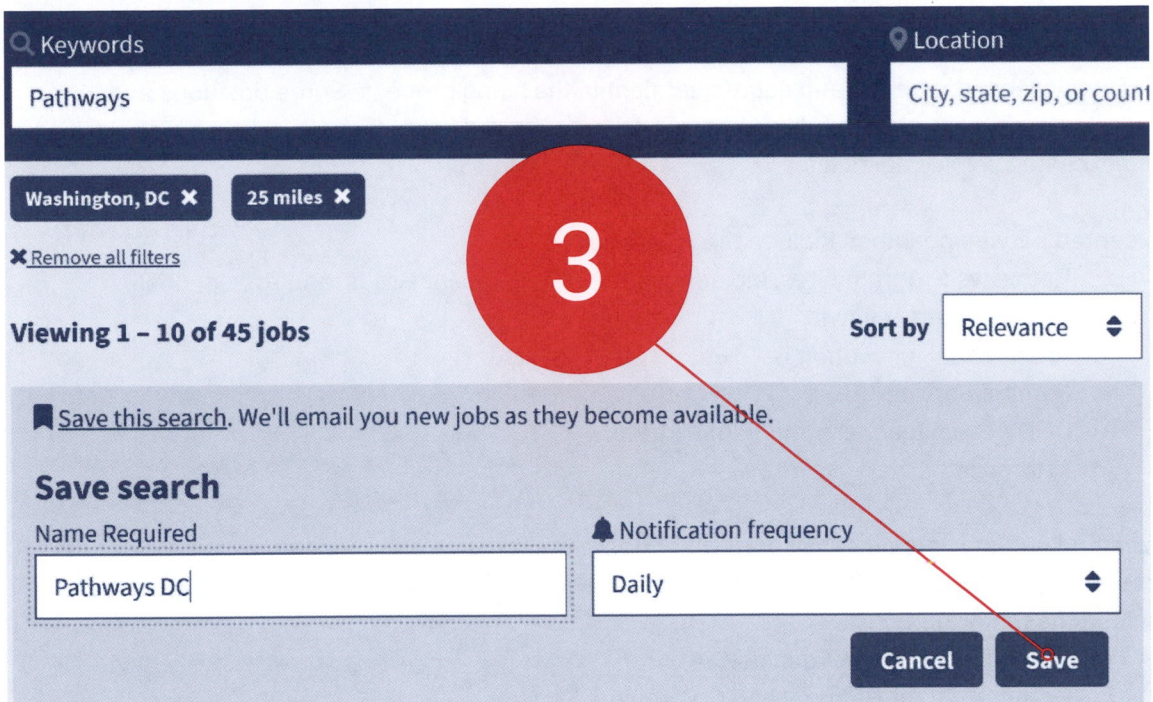

Search for jobs (not just Internships) at the grade level you are seeking.

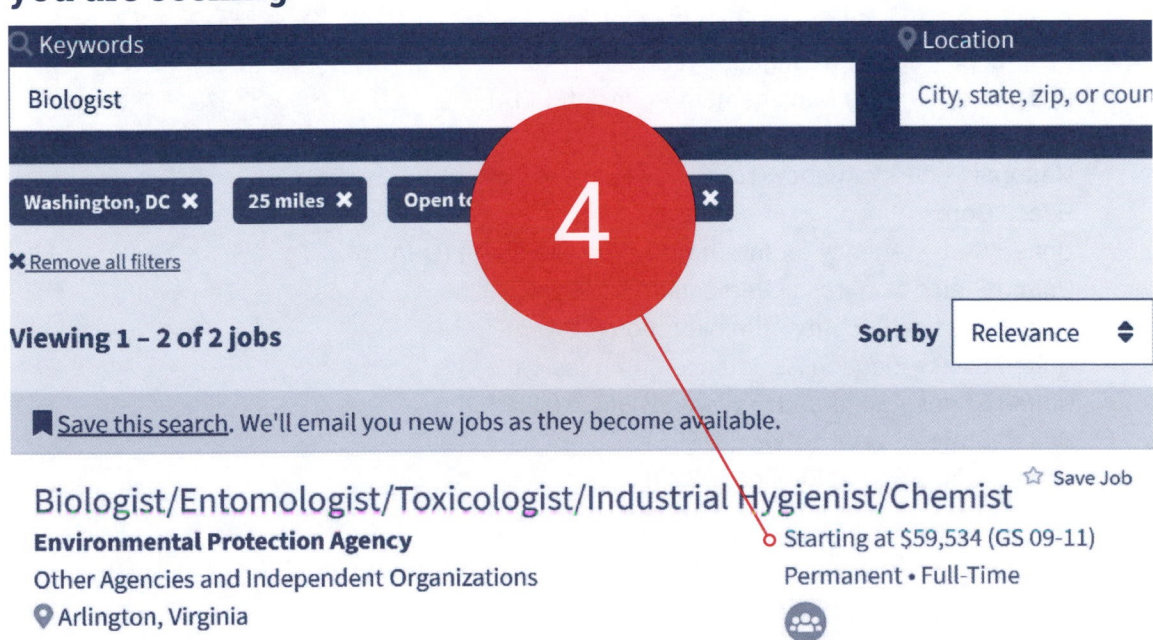

Excepted Service Agencies

Most Federal jobs are part of the competitive service and follow rules to ensure that applicants and employees receive fair and equal treatment in the hiring process. Some positions and agencies are excepted from following these same rules and are called excepted service positions and excepted service agencies.

Excepted service positions include the following:
*   ★ Pathways Program hires, including internships, Recent Grads, and Presidential Management Fellows
*   ★ Presidential Innovation Fellows
*   ★ Foreign Service
*   ★ DOD school teachers and administrators
*   ★ Attorneys

Excepted service agencies may or may not post their vacancy announcements on USAJOBS. You may need to check the websites of these agencies to find their job postings. Examples include the following:
*   ★ Central Intelligence Agency (CIA)
*   ★ Corporation for National and Community Service
*   ★ Defense Intelligence Agency (DIA)
*   ★ Department of Defense Cyber Excepted Service (CES)
*   ★ Federal Air Marshal Service (FAMS)
*   ★ Federal Aviation Administration (FAA)
*   ★ Federal Bureau of Investigation (FBI)
*   ★ Federal Emergency Management Agency (FEMA)
*   ★ Federal Reserve Board
*   ★ National Security Agency (NSA)
*   ★ Peace Corps
*   ★ United States Agency for International Development (USAID)
*   ★ United States Congress - Personal Office Staff
*   ★ Transportation Security Administration (TSA)
*   ★ United States Election Assistance Commission
*   ★ United States Patent and Trademark Office (USPTO)
*   ★ United States Postal Service (USPS)
*   ★ United States Secret Service (USSS)

> Many of these agencies do not post their positions on USAJOBS.

Direct Hire Authority / Job Fairs

Direct Hire

Direct Hire Authority (DHA) for Post-Secondary Students and Recent Graduates of 2017
The Federal government may hire qualified recent graduates non-competitively into competitive service positions, into limited numbers of professional and administrative positions at the GS-11 level or below. The law also allows non-competitive hiring of qualified current students under the same requirements into temporary positions, with an option for the agency to convert them to competitive service positions.

DHA for Post-Secondary Students and Recent Graduates (authority expires September 30, 2025, unless extended by future legislation), Interns and Recent Graduates from Post-Secondary Institutions of Higher Education.

What this means for you
The Federal agency recruiters might have direct hire positions. The best way to be considered for direct hire is to attend a job fair with a 3-4 page resume that describes your experience in some depth. If you are a student who was hired non-competitively into a temporary position, your agency may convert your temporary position into a permanent position.

IMPORTANT UPDATE: The government is currently exploring whether or not to extend direct hire authority to Science, Technology, Engineering, and Mathematics (STEM) and cybersecurity occupations. Be on the lookout for this potential hiring change!

Positions in the Cyber Workforce (as defined in DoD Directive 8140.01, Cyberspace Workforce Management, designated with a cyber work role code)

Positions in the Acquisition Workforce that are responsible for managing any services contracts necessary to the operation and maintenance of programs of the DoD

Positions in financial management, accounting, auditing, actuary, cost estimation, operational research, business, or business administration for which a qualified candidate possess a finance, accounting, management, actuarial science, or related degree from an accredited college or university, or equivalent experience relevant to the functions of the position being filled

---

Coronavirus (COVID-19)

IMPORTANT UPDATE: COVID-19 Federal jobs for Recent Graduates and Students are available and are DIRECT HIRE.

Job Fairs: Top Tips

★ Bring copies of your 2-4 page Federal resume to the job fair. Do not take a 1-page resume for any consideration of being hired, because it cannot be done.

★ Expand your work experience descriptions.

★ Accomplishments should be specific, quantifiable, visible, and interesting for the HR recruiter to see the skills and abilities that you have.

★ List your relevant college courses in your education section.

★ Make a list of your skills in a separate section on page one.

★ Be prepared to speak with an HR person. It's helpful to know what kind of job you're applying for and to do some research on USAJOBS about Federal positions.

> The Post-Secondary Direct Hire Authority is used at college and other job fairs regularly. Be prepared -- you could be HIRED DIRECTLY as a result of a Job Fair.

WE'RE HIRING!

STEP 04 Vacancy Announcements and Keywords

Keywords from the job announcement could be the key to your success with your Federal resume.

establishing relationships · radiological health · conduct studies · giving feedback · funding recommendations · provide leadership · cross-cultural · ensure compliance · integrate technology · monitoring · enhance performance · embedded systems · administration · interpret data · computer engineering · propose · review research · explain procedures · provide consulation · cloud computing · integration · skills · interpersonal · coordinates research · conducts inquiries · peer review · instruct · fund · mentor · technical guidance · maintain security · comprehensive reports · establish deadlines · lead discussions · population dynamics · minimize failures · communication · review · coordination · networks · formulate policies · content editing · model data · simulations · decision making · exchange information · statistical techniques · plans · presenting data · technical reports · conducts audits · collaborating · technical consultation · assess costs · validate · interferential predictions · multivariate analysis inspections · negotiate · recovery plans · spatial patterns · time management · additive models · interagency communication · leadership · review applications · design patterns · cybersecurity · future challanges · field sampling · inclusitivity · interpret results · primary advisor · systems analyses · conduct appraisals · investigations · formulate approaches · managing requests · publish results · develop tools · surveying areas · establish partnerships · compiling data · oversee policy · resolve problems · track compliance · test protocols · gain expertise · community structure · scientific research

Vacancy Announcements and Keywords

This step will cover keywords in three types of vacancy announcements:
1. Pathways Internships
2. Pathways Recent Graduates
3. Entry level Federal positions (GS 5/7/9)

Don't get intimidated: just read the sections in the announcement and MATCH your resume to the QUALIFICATIONS in the announcement. If you study the announcement and match your resume, you could get BEST QUALIFIED.

The most important sections of a USAJOBS announcement to review and match your resume will be:

★ Qualifications-Specialized Experience
★ Education-major and/or courses required
★ How You Will Be Evaluated – may have required core competencies or Knowledge, Skills, and Abilities (KSAs)
★ Online self-assessment questionnaire

Critical Vacancy Announcement Features

Follow the Directions!
Be sure to study these sections on every announcement so that you can successfully follow the directions. **Examples of these sections are on the following pages.**

Closing Dates
Read this immediately! An announcement may be open for as few as 5 days, or it may close after an agency receives a set number of applications. Other announcements may state **"Open Continuously,"** **"Inventory Building,"** or **"12 Month Roster."**

Who May Apply?
This section will state the **types of applicants** who may be considered for the position.

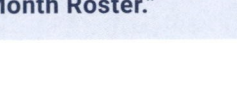

Duties
This section describes what tasks you will be performing if you are hired. **Note that this section does NOT have the best keywords for your resume.**

Qualifications
Are you qualified? Read the **SPECIALIZED EXPERIENCE** in the Qualifications section to find out. This section is the **BEST FOR KEYWORDS** for your Federal resume. Also read this section for **EDUCATION REQUIREMENTS**. Be sure to feature the education, courses, and major(s) in your Federal resume.

Knowledge, Skills, and Abilities (KSAs)
If KSAs are listed in the announcement, they are the **CRITICAL KEYWORDS** that you will need to cover in your Federal resume. Follow the Outline Format resume examples in this book to highlight KSAs in your resume.

How You Will be Evaluated
This section describes how the agency will determine who will be considered **Best Qualified for the position.**

How to Apply and Documents
Pay attention here; these instructions are different for each announcement and must be followed exactly. **Read the instructions for required documents.** Pathways Internships and Recent Graduates must upload a copy of transcripts. If hired, you may be required to send an official copy of your transcript.

Questionnaires
Beware, this is a TEST! You need a score of 90 to 95. Give yourself all the credit that you can. Reflect your answers in your Federal resume; Human Resources will read your resume to see if it matches your answers to the questions.

STUDENT'S **FEDERAL CAREER GUIDE**

47

How to Read Vacancy Announcements

Follow the Directions!

Be sure to study these sections on every announcement so that you can successfully follow the directions. Each USAJOBS announcement is the similar, but slightly different. See samples of the important sections of the announcements here.

Closing Dates

If the announcement looks good, always look at closing date quickly to see the deadline. It could be TOMORROW! Time your application development to meet the deadlines!

An announcement may be open for as few as 5 days, or it may close after an agency receives a set number of applications. Other announcements may stay open for a year or more; these agencies are collecting resumes for current and future openings in many locations. Apply for these positions!

Open & closing dates

🕐 02/21/2020 to 03/01/2020

This job will close when we have received **100 applications** which may be sooner than the closing date. Learn more

This Job Is Open To

This section will state the types of applicants who may be considered for the position. Look for the ones applicable to you, such as **Students, Recent Graduates, Public, Veterans, Competitive.**

This job is open to

 Students
Current students enrolled in accredited educational institutions from high school to graduate level. Includes internships, pathways and other student programs.

Clarification from the agency

Direct Hire Authority for Post-Secondary Students. Applicants may be selected at the GS-03 or GS-04 grade levels with promotion potential to the GS-11.

> This GREAT announcement has both Direct Hire Authority and promotion potential to a GS-11.

This job is open to

 Recent graduates
Individuals who have graduated from an accredited educational institute or certificate program within the last 2 years or 6 years for Veterans.

 The public
U.S. citizens, nationals or those who owe allegiance to the U.S.

> Non-veterans have 2 years from graduation and veterans have 6 years from graduation to apply for Recent Graduate announcement.

Clarification from the agency

U.S. Citizens; Individuals who have graduated from an accredited educational institute or certificate program within the last 2 years or 4 years for veterans

Duties

In Duties, look for the responsibilities of the position. Read this description to help yourself decide if this is the job for you. NOTE: This is NOT the best section for your keywords.

DON PATHWAYS RECENT GRADUATE GENERAL ENGINEER

Pay scale & grade	**Salary**
GS 7 - 9	$48,670 to $77,396 per yea

Appointment type	**Work schedule**
Permanent	Full-Time

DON Recent Graduates Program. You will serve as a General Engineer in the NAVSUP Energy Office Engineering Division of CNSSC OPERATIONAL SUPPORT FIELD.

Responsibilities
- You will assist in facilitating projects from planning through execution stages.
- You will interact with other governmental agencies and private contractors.
- You will participate in multi-agency meetings to develop planning requirements, technical specifications, and standard practices.
- You will provide expertise and support for projects.
- You will submit data and project status to management.

The Best Keywords for the Outline Format Federal Resume are found in the Qualifications Section!

GS-07:

> GS-07 is more general, easier to get Best Qualified

KNOWLEDGE OF GENERAL ENGINEERING PRACTICES AND METHODOLOGY
KNOWLEDGE OF OPERATIONS, MAINTENANCE, DESIGN OF WORKING FACILITIES
ASSIST ENGINEERS WITH IDENTIFYING FUTURE FACILITY NEEDS
RESOLVE ENGINEERING PROBLEM-SOLVING
COMMUNICATE AND WRITE BOTH TECHNICAL AND NON-TECHNICAL INFORMATION

> GS-09 position is specific for Fuel Facilities Projects!

GS-09:

KNOWLEDGE OF GENERAL ENGINEERING PRACTICES AND METHODOLOGY
KNOWLEDGE OF OPERATIONS AND DESIGN OF PETROLEUM FACILITIES
IDENTIFY FACILITY NEEDS, DEVELOP SCOPE AND COSS
INTERACT WITH AGENCIES REGARDING FUEL FACILITY PROJECTS
REVIEW AND MAINTAIN OVERSIGHT OF FUEL FACILITY PROJECTS
ADD FOR BOTH GRADE LEVELS:
ENGINEERING PROJECT MANAGEMENT
- ORAL COMMUNICATION
- PARTNERING
- WRITTEN COMMUNICATION

Qualifications

Are you qualified? Read the SPECIALIZED EXPERIENCE in the Qualifications section to find out. This section is the BEST FOR KEYWORDS for your Federal resume. Also read this section for EDUCATION REQUIREMENTS. Be sure to feature the education, courses, and major(s) in your Federal resume.

DON PATHWAYS RECENT GRADUATE GENERAL ENGINEER

Qualifications

GS-07: Your resume must demonstrate at least one year of specialized experience at or equivalent to the GS-05 grade level or pay band in the Federal service or equivalent experience in the private or public sector applying a *knowledge of professional general engineering practices, methodology, principles, theories, precedents, concepts, and techniques associated with the operation, maintenance, and design of working facilities.* **Examples of specialized experience include: 1) Assist higher-level engineers with identifying future facility needs; 2) Assist in projects to resolve engineering problems; 3) Communicate orally and in writing to convey technical and non-technical information.**

GS-09: Your resume must demonstrate at least one year of specialized experience at or equivalent to the GS-07 grade level or pay band in the Federal service or equivalent experience in the private or public sector as a *professional applying knowledge of professional general engineering practices, methodology, principles, theories, precedents, concepts, and techniques associated with the operation, maintenance, and design of petroleum facilities.* **Examples of specialized experience include: 1) Identify future facility needs, development of scope, cost estimate, and project data; 2) Interact with other agencies in regards to fuel facility projects and activities; 3) Review and maintain close oversight of approved fuel facility projects.**

How You Will Be Evaluated

You will be evaluated for this job based on how well you meet the qualifications above. In order to qualify for this position, your resume must provide sufficient experience and/or education, knowledge, skills, and abilities to perform the duties of the specific position for which you are being considered. Your resume is the key means we have for evaluating your skills, knowledge, and abilities as they relate to this position. Therefore, we encourage you to be clear and specific when describing your experience.

ENGINEERING PROJECT MANAGEMENT
- **ORAL COMMUNICATION**
- **PARTNERING**
- **WRITTEN COMMUNICATION**

Knowledge, Skills, and Abilities (KSAs)

If KSAs are listed in the announcement, they are the CRITICAL KEYWORDS that you will need to cover in your Federal resume. Follow the Outline Format resume examples in this book to highlight KSAs as headings in your work experience descriptions and add accomplishments that will demonstrate your KSAs.

KNOWLEDGE, SKILLS AND ABILITIES (KSAs): Your qualifications will be evaluated on the basis of your level of knowledge, skills, abilities and/or competencies in the following areas:

1. Knowledge of analytical and evaluative methods and techniques for assessing program development or execution and improving organizational effectiveness and efficiency.
2. Knowledge of management principles and processes.
3. Skill in application of fact finding and investigative techniques.
4. Ability to communicate orally and in writing.
5. Ability to develop presentations and reports.

> QUIZ – For the KSAs above, circle the keywords that you would want to add to your Federal resume.

KNOWLEDGE, SKILLS AND ABILITIES (KSAs): Your qualifications will be evaluated on the basis of your level of knowledge, skills, abilities and/or competencies in the following areas:

1. Knowledge of environmental engineering principles and concepts needed for application to a wide range of environmental situation in designing and planning for Air Quality, Water Quality, Asbestos, Lead Based Paint, Toxic Substance Controls, Pollution Prevention, Hazardous Waste, Solid Waste, Above/Underground Storage Tanks, and Permit Management.
2. Familiarity with related engineering fields such as mechanical, chemical, civil or electrical as they apply to the specialty area.
3. Knowledge of policies, objectives, needs and practices applicable to the full range of duties concerned with the operation, maintenance and modification of pollution abatement facilities.
4. Knowledge and skill to assess the impact of the installation's activities on public safety, ecology and environment.
5. Knowledge of Environmental Regulations including Federal, State and Local regulatory requirements.

How You Will Be Evaluated

This section describes how the agency will determine who will be considered Best Qualified for the position, and may include information about category ratings, core competencies, KSAs, or even a link for more information.

How You Will Be Evaluated

You will be evaluated for this job based on how well you meet the qualifications above.

IN DESCRIBING YOUR EXPERIENCE, PLEASE BE CLEAR AND SPECIFIC. WE WILL NOT MAKE ASSUMPTIONS REGARDING YOUR EXPERIENCE.

Narrative responses are not required at this time. If you are referred for consideration, you may be asked to submit additional job related information, which may include, but not limited to; responses to the knowledge, skills and abilities; completion of a work sample, and/or contact for an interview. Your resume and/or supporting documentation will be verified. Please follow all instructions carefully. Errors or omissions may affect your rating or consideration for employment.

Vacancy Announcements and Keywords

How You Will Be Evaluated

You will be evaluated for this job based on how well you meet the qualifications above.

Once the announcement has closed, a review of your application package (resume, supporting documents, and responses to the questionnaire) will be used to determine whether you meet the qualification requirements listed on this announcement. If you are minimally qualified, your résumé and supporting documentation will be compared against your responses to the assessment questionnaire to determine your level of experience. If, after reviewing your résumé and/or supporting documentation, a determination is made that you have inflated your qualifications and/or experience, you may lose consideration for this position. Please follow all instructions carefully when applying, errors or omissions may affect your eligibility.

You should list any relevant performance appraisals and incentive awards in your resume as that information may be taken into consideration during the selection process. If selected, you may be required to provide supporting documentation.

How You Will Be Evaluated

You will be evaluated for this job based on how well you meet the qualifications above.

The U.S. Department of the Treasury has a distinguished history dating back to the founding of our nation. As the steward of U.S. economic and financial systems, Treasury is a major and influential leader in today's global economy. We have over 100,000 employees across the country and around the world. Come Join the Department of the Treasury and Invest in Tomorrow.

Your application includes your resume, responses to the online questions, and required supporting documents. Please be sure that your resume includes detailed information to support your qualifications for this position; failure to provide sufficient evidence in your resume may result in a "not qualified" determination.

Rating: Your application will be evaluated in the following areas: **Teamwork, Oral and Written Communication, Information Resources Strategy & Planning, Information Systems Network Security, Project Management.** Category rating will be used to rank and select eligible candidates. If qualified, you will be assigned to one of three quality level categories, (i.e., A = Superior, B = Highly Qualified, C= Qualified) depending on your responses to the online questions, regarding your experience, education, and training related to this position. Your rating may be lowered if your responses to the online questions are not supported by the education and/or experience described in your application. Veterans' preference is applied after applicants are assessed. Preference-eligibles will be listed at the top of their assigned category and considered before non-preference-eligibles in that category. Qualified preference-eligibles with a compensable service-connected disability of 10% or more will be listed at the top of the highest category.

Referral: If you are among the top qualified candidates, your application may be referred to a selecting official for consideration. You may be required to participate in a selection interview (telephonic and/or in person at the discretion of the Selecting Official in accordance with hiring polices). We will not reimburse costs related to the interview such as travel to and from the interview site.

QUIZ – In the "Rating" section above, circle the keywords that you would want to add to your Federal resume.

Required Documents

Pay attention here! Read the instructions for required documents. These must be followed exactly. Pathways Internships and Recent Graduates must upload a copy of transcripts. If hired, you may be required to send an official copy of your transcript.

Required Documents

The documents you are required to submit vary based on whether or not you are eligible for preference in federal employment. A complete description of preference categories and the associated required documents is in the Applicant Checklist (External).

1. Your resume:

Your resume may be submitted in any format and must support the specialized experience described in this announcement.

If your resume includes a photograph or other inappropriate material or content, it will not be used to make eligibility and qualification determinations and you may not be considered for this vacancy.

For qualifications determinations your resume must contain hours worked per week and the dates of employment (i.e., HRS per week and month/year to month/year or month/year to present). If your resume does not contain this information, your application may be marked as incomplete and you may not receive consideration for this position.

For additional information see: What to include in your resume.

2. Transcripts and Enrollment Verification:

Enrollment verification (if transcripts do not reflect current enrollment), and unofficial transcripts for education claimed in your resume and occupational questionnaire is required. If you provide an unofficial transcript at the time of application and you are selected, you will be asked for official versions prior to appointment. See: Transcripts and Licenses

3. Other supporting documents:

Cover Letter, optional

Required Documents

A complete application includes 1. A resume, 2. Vacancy question responses, 3. Provide proof of enrollment or education (see education documentation required) and 4. Submission of any required documents. Please note that if you do not provide all required information, as specified in this announcement, you will not be considered for this position (or may not receive the special consideration for which you may be eligible).

All applicants are required to submit a resume either by creating one in USAJOBS or uploading one of their own choosing. (Cover letters are optional). To receive full credit for relevant experience, please list the month/year and number of hours worked for experience listed on your resume. We suggest that you preview the online questions, as you may need to customize your resume to ensure that it supports your responses to these questions. Please view Resume Tips

VETERANS' PREFERENCE DOCUMENTATION: If you are claiming veterans' preference, you must submit a copy of your DD-214 (Member 4 copy), or other official documentation from a branch of the Armed Forces or the Department of Veterans Affairs showing dates of service and type of discharge. Ten-point preference eligibles must also submit an Application for 10-point Veteran Preference, SF-15, along with the required documentation listed on the back of the SF-15 form. For more information on veterans' preference view **FedsHireVets.**

EDUCATION DOCUMENTATION: You must submit dated documentation showing completion or intended completion(if graduation is no more than 9 months from the date of application) of all educational requirements (e.g. letter from the registrar, unofficial transcripts). An official transcript will be required if you are selected.A college or university degree generally must be from an accredited (or pre-accredited) college or university recognized by the U.S. Department of Education.For a list of schools which meet these criteria,please refer to Department of Education Accreditation page. If you are qualifying based on foreign education, you must submit proof of creditability of education as evaluated by a credentialing agency. Refer to the OPM instructions. If you are qualifying based on a certificate program, please refer to the Treasury's Pathways Program page for more information on qualifying certificate programs..

If you are relying on your education to meet qualification requirements:

Education must be accredited by an accrediting institution recognized by the U.S. Department of Education in order for it to be credited towards qualifications. Therefore, provide only the attendance and/or degrees from schools accredited by accrediting institutions recognized by the U.S. Department of Education.

Failure to provide all of the required information as stated in this vacancy announcement may result in an ineligible rating or may affect the overall rating.

How to Apply

Pay attention here! These instructions are different for each announcement and must be followed exactly.

How to Apply

To apply for this position, you must complete the online questionnaire and submit the documentation specified in the **Required Documents** section below.

The complete application package must be submitted by 11:59 PM (EST) on 12/31/2020 to receive consideration

To begin, click **Apply** to access the online application. You will need to be logged into your USAJOBS account to apply. If you do not have a USAJOBS account, you will need to create one before beginning the application (https://apply.usastaffing.gov/ViewQuestionnaire/10449805).

Follow the prompts to **select your résumé and/or other supporting documents** to be included with your application package. You will have the opportunity to upload additional documents to include in your application before it is submitted. Your uploaded documents may take several hours to clear the virus scan process.

After acknowledging you have reviewed your application package, complete the Include Personal Information section as you deem appropriate and **click to continue with the application process**.

You will be taken to the online application which you must complete in order to apply for the position. Complete the online application, verify the required documentation is included with your application package, and submit the application. **You must re-select your resume and/or other documents from your USAJOBS account or your application will be incomplete**.

It is your responsibility to verify that your application package (resume, supporting documents, and responses to the questionnaire) is complete, accurate, and submitted by the closing date. Uploaded documents may take up to one hour to clear the virus scan.

Additional information on how to complete the online application process and submit your online application may be found on the USA Staffing Applicant Resource Center.

To verify the status of your application, log into your USAJOBS account (https://my.usajobs.gov/Account/Login), all of your applications will appear on the Welcome screen. The Application Status will appear along with the date your application was last updated. For information on what each Application Status means, visit: https://www.usajobs.gov/Help/how-to/application/status/.

How to Apply

Please send all application materials to:

FJCInternProgramITO@fjc.gov

> Sometimes for internships that are not posted on USAJOBS, you send application materials to an email.

Fall Semester dates: September - December: Fall Semester application deadline: mid June

Spring Semester dates: January - April: Spring Semester application deadline: mid October

Summer Semester dates: May - August: Summer Semester application Deadline: mid March

WE'RE HIRING!

Questionnaires: Beware, this is a TEST! You need a score of 90 to 100%.

You need to get the highest score possible. Rate yourself the highest possible based on your courses, papers, projects, internships, jobs, and volunteer activities.

> There are 20 questions and you have to try to get a score of 90 or above. You will have to base your answers on education, courses, internships or work history.

For each item, select the one response that most accurately describes your current level of experience and capability using the scale below.

6. **Analyze accounting records, documents, and other relevant information through transaction testing to assure compliance with accounting principles, operating procedures, and laws and regulations.**
   - A. I do not have experience or demonstrated capability in performing this activity, but I am willing to learn.
   - B. I have limited experience in performing this activity. I have had exposure to this activity but would require additional guidance, instruction, or experience to perform it at a satisfactory level.
   - C. I have a fair amount of experience and a fair amount of demonstrated capability in performing this activity. I can perform this activity satisfactorily but could benefit from additional guidance, instruction, or experience to perform this activity more effectively.
   - D. I have considerable experience and considerable demonstrated capability in performing this activity. I can perform this activity independently and effectively.
   - ● E. I have extensive experience and extensive demonstrated capability in performing this activity. I am considered an expert; _**I am able to train or assist others; and my work is typically not reviewed by a supervisor.**_ I have received verbal and/or written recognition from others in carrying out this activity.

> E is the best answer here.

7. Assist with fact finding studies to obtain or verify financial information.
8. Review a general ledger and subsidiary ledgers to account for transactions.
9. Review financial work papers for compliance with operating procedures and practices.
10. Use prescribed formulas, schedules or procedures to calculate/check routine values.
11. Compile financial information from files to input into databases and spreadsheets.
12. Edit financial reports for format, math, and document integrity to ensure accuracy of final report.
13. Use automated system or database to sort, calculate, and retrieve data for preparation of spreadsheets or reports.
14. Analyze records, documents, and other information to verify accuracy.
15. Apply policy and procedures to develop conclusions regarding financial data.
16. Identify needs or problems and determine corrective action.

Promotion Potential

Look for vacancy announcements with promotion potential, which shows the highest grade you could be promoted to without further competition. You may be promoted to the next level if you have performed at the lower grade for at least one year; performed at an acceptable level of competence; and demonstrated an ability to work at the next higher grade level. In this example below, a person hired into this position at GS-9 could be promoted each year to GS-11, GS-12, and finally GS-13, without further competition.

IRS Pathways Recent Graduate Program (Management and Program Analyst)

DEPARTMENT OF TREASURY

<u>Internal Revenue Service</u>

Human Capital Office

Overview

Open & closing dates

🕐 05/15/2020 to 05/29/2020

Pay scale & grade

GS 5 - 9

Appointment type

Recent Graduates

Promotion Potential

12

Service

Competitive

Salary

$34,916 to $83,897 per year

Work schedule

Full-Time

If selected, you will be placed in a developmental position as a Management and Program Analyst, GS-0343-05 with promotion potential to GS-12in one the division(s) listed below:

Appeals
Human Capital Office
Large Business and International
Research, Applied Analytics and Statistics
Wage and Investment
Procurement

If you land this position, you can start at GS 5; one year to GS 7; one year to GS 9; one year to GS 11; one year to GS 12. From 5 to 12 in 5 years! No promises, but this could happen. You need good evaluations!

STEP 05 Basic Federal Resume

Your basic Federal resume must have some required information. A good way to start is to fill out the required fields in the USAJOBS Resume Builder, then download the text to build your competitive Federal resume in Step 6. Or follow the checklist below to get started.

EDUCATION

WORK EXPERIENCE

Checklist for Your Basic Federal Resume

PERSONAL INFORMATION

Full name
Mailing address (with zip code)
Phone number with area code
Email

EDUCATION

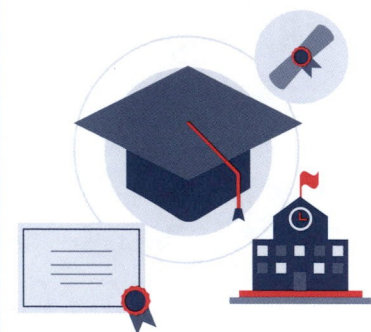

Colleges, universities, and high school

Name of school(s), **city, state, and zip code**

Major(s)

Type and year of any degrees received

(If no degree was received, show total credits earned and indicate whether semester or quarter hours.)

Professional training, workshops, certification training

WORK HISTORY

Job title (include series and grade if it was a Federal job)

Employer's name and specific address, city, state, and zip code

Starting and ending dates (month and year)

Hours per week

Salary (optional, not required)

Supervisor's name and phone number (if you have this information)

Permission (if you choose) **to contact your current supervisor**
(Saying "no" is acceptable and will not affect your chances of being considered for the position.)

Duties

Sample Basic Federal Resume

SAVANNAH A. SMITH

12 Cedar Court, Pasadena, CA 94502 (510) 333-3333 • Savannahsmith7@yahoo.com

EXPERIENCE

AUGUST 2018 TO MAY 2019
INDEPENDENT RESEARCH PROJECT, SONOMA STATE UNIVERSITY

Managed research team that developed processes that reduced brewery wastewater organics prior to discharge. Final project data resulted in local brewery reviewing wastewater disposal protocols that reduced organics and chemical oxygen demand prior to discharge into the wastewater treatment plant system. Documented and analyzed data on Excel. Research findings presented at the 2019 Sonoma State University's Science Symposium.

AUGUST 2014 TO MAY 2019
LABORATORY TEACHING ASSISTANT, SONOMA STATE UNIVERSITY AND CHABOT COMMUNITY COLLEGE

Provided hands-on instruction and oversight to lower and upper level students in setup and use of laboratory equipment to include light and fluorescence microscopes, vermifilters, peristaltic pumps, plating, safety procedures, and proper laboratory techniques.

EDUCATION

MAY 2019
BACHELOR OF SCIENCE IN BIOLOGY, SONOMA STATE UNIVERSITY

Achieved the Bachelor of Science in Biology with a concentration of Molecular and Cellular Biology with a minor in Chemistry. Multiyear member of Biology Club and Student Health Advisory Committee.

JUNE 2012
HIGH SCHOOL DIPLOMA, ALAMEDA HIGH SCHOOL

SKILLS

- Highly proficient following SOPs, laboratory standards, and performing aseptic techniques.
- Highly detail, self-motivating, process orientated, & self-reliant.
- Key understanding of Electronic Document Management Systems (EDMS) & BOX.

- Extensive laboratory experience in isolating, culturing, and analyzing fungal spores and bacteria.
- Highly proficient in Adobe Acrobat Professional, Microsoft Excel, Outlook, PowerPoint, and Word.
- Essential understanding of records management and lifecycle procedures.

REFERENCES

Dr. James Smith
Affiliation: Mentor for Independent Research Project at Sonoma State University
Contact: jsmith@gmail.com Phone Number: (777) 777-7777

Janette Jones
Affiliation: PLM Analyst at Eurofins
Contact: janettejones@gmail.com
Phone Number: (202) 777-7777

SUCCESS STORY

SAVANNAH'S – TARGET CONSUMER SAFETY OFFICER, GS-7
JOB SEARCH… April 1 to May 15, 2020

Dear Kathryn,
I got news on Thursday that I was tentatively eligible for the GS-7 position and that my application was referred to the hiring manager in White Oaks, MD.

+++++++++++++++++++++++++++++++

Hey Kathryn!

Thank you so much! I really appreciate it! The in-person interview lasted about an hour and it actually went better than expected!

Thank you so much for the tips! I really appreciate it! Yes, the specificity of my experience HELPED a lot. Especially using examples both at my current position and at school. I was able to interchange them back and forth.

Will do! The next update would be in about 3-4 weeks or so! Let's see what happens. They take their sweet time alright! Of course, it really means a lot!

+++++++++++++++++++++++++++++++

Yes, I did get news from the FDA offering me a tentative position for Consumer Safety Officer (GS-7) on the 19th. We're further coordinating for a security clearance appointment. It was originally going to be on the 8th, but due to the virus, it got postponed. I'll get a response from them when I will be able to schedule an appointment. I pretty much filled out the forms, just missing one form to fill out. I'm still tackling the Cyber Security Awareness training, since it's a bigger training module than I thought it was. Just waiting for the next step.

+++++++++++++++++++++++++++++++

Dear Savannah,
Congratulations!
All of your pre-employment and security requirements are complete, and we are delighted to extend a <u>final offer of employment</u> with the Department of Health and Human Services, Food and Drug Administration, Office of Regulatory Affairs, San Francisco District Office, located in Alameda, California.

STEP 06 Best Federal Resume Format

Now that you have a basic Federal resume, follow these steps to turn it into a Federal resume that can get you noticed and hired.

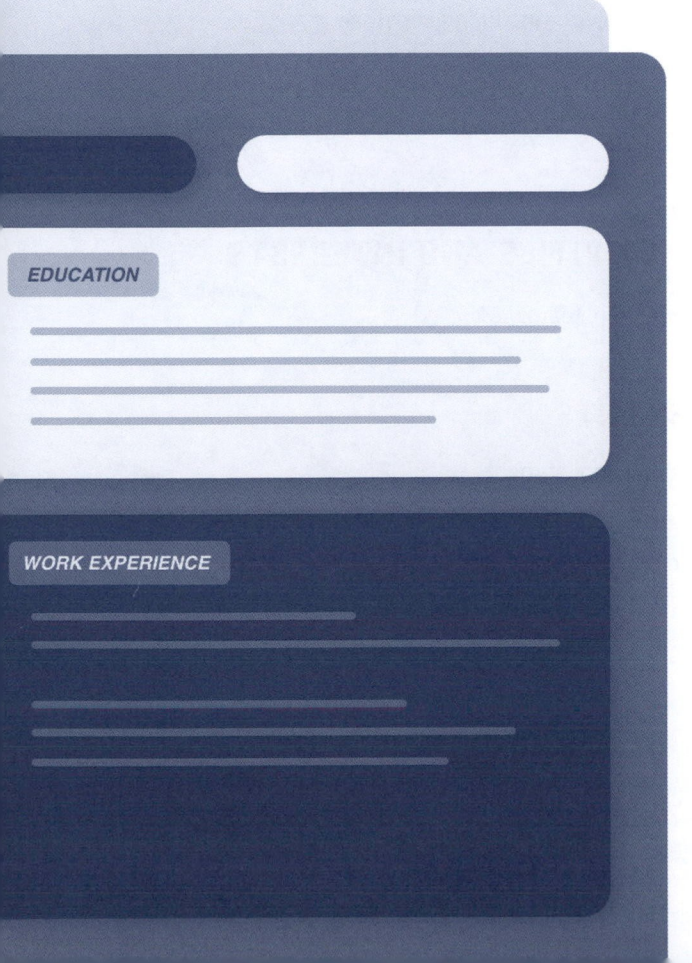

EDUCATION

WORK EXPERIENCE

PROJECTS

INTERNSHIP

VOLUNTEERING

How to Turn Your Basic Federal Resume Into a Competitive Federal Resume

Basic **Resume**

Competitve Federal **Resume**

 TARGET: 2 TO 4 PAGES IN LENGTH

 ### OUTLINE FORMAT

Use **KEYWORDS** from the vacancy announcement as **ALL CAPS** headings for work history descriptions and college projects

 ### EDUCATION / COURSEWORK

Relevant, major courses and credit hours

Significant papers and projects, including capstone, major engineering, or science projects

Thesis, methods, and outcomes

GPA if 3.5 or above

 ### VOLUNTEER ACTIVITIES AND INTERESTS

Hobbies, sports, leadership, teamwork

 ### ACCOMPLISHMENTS

Work and internship accomplishments

Course projects

Honors, awards, and recognitions

 ### SKILLS

List your technical and specific skills, such as software, hardware, research, data management, writing / editing, communications.

Outline Format Federal Resume

The Outline Format resume was developed by Kathryn Troutman in 1996 for the first edition of the *Federal Resume Guidebook*. This format is still preferred by Federal Human Resources specialists because it is easy to read and rate. It is important to always remember that Federal resumes submitted through USAJOBS are read, reviewed, and rated by Human Resources Specialists—not by an automated system. The following example provides an introduction into how a single job block written in the Outline Format should look. Keep in mind that this is just one job block from a resume. This approach outlines your knowledge, skills, and abilities in an easy-to-read and easy-to-rate format that makes it simple for the Human Resources Specialist to identify what you bring to the table.

---

(1)

EDUCATION

University of Maryland Baltimore County (UMBC), Baltimore, MD 21250. Completed 151 semester hours in a BS degree program in Computer Science (Minor: Statistics and Economics) (GPA: 3.17/4.0). Expected graduation: December 2020. *Relevant coursework*:

Computer Science: Computer Science I for Majors, Discrete Structures, Social/Ethical Issues in IT, Computer Organization & Assembly Language, Principles of Programming Languages, Data Structures, Computer Architecture, Principles of Operating Systems, Software Engineering I, Database Management Systems, Artificial Intelligence

Economics: Principles of Microeconomics, Principles of Macroeconomics, Intermediate Microeconomic Analysis, Intermediate Macroeconomic Analysis, Benefit-Cost Evaluation, Economics of Natural Resources, Health Economics

Statistics: Introduction to Statistics, Probability & Statistics for **(2)** and Engineering, Time Series Data Analysis, Introduction to Probability Theory, Applied Statistics

ACADEMIC PROJECTS

- **Academic Coding Project** - *Building Linux Shell in C,* 250 Lines of Code (LOC) (CMSC421/ Principles of Operating Systems): Designed a shell for Linux that supports a few basic features of a full-fledge *nix shell. The shell presents the user with a command prompt; accepts a command input of an arbitrary length; parses command-line arguments from the user's input; and passes them to the user defined program. The application was not allowed to use any external libraries other than the system's C library (2018).

JOB EXPERIENCE

IT Consultant (09/2019 – Present)
ROUTE 144 CLASSIFIED
P.O. Box 21275, Baltimore, MD 21228
Part-Time: 10 hours/week
Base Salary: $15.00/hour
Supervisor: Darryl Phillips, (410) 111-2222; *May contact*

(3) DATA ANALYSIS Complete data analysis and market research studies pertinent to the publication needs of a local classified advertising publication. Manage the advertisement ordering process, from order receipt to publication. Validate and reconcile advertising sales invoices.

ACCOMPLISHMENT: Compiled pertinent employment, sales, and other customer-centric metrics. Designed and developed Excel pivot tables to highlight trends and produced informative business forecasts with the goal to increase sales.

---

(1) Put your education first, if recent.

(2) Add descriptions of your projects and major papers.

(3) ALL CAPS headlines for each paragraph using KEYWORDS from the announcement

(4) Add your accomplishments at the end of each job block.

Resume sample: **Greg Martinez** IT Specialist, Information Assurance, GS-2210-07
BS, Computer Science, Minor: Statistics and Economics

Competitive Student Federal Resume Example

HIRED BY THE FDA!

See how the basic resume example in Step 5 is transformed into a competitive student Federal resume by using the Outline Format.

SAVANNAH A. SMITH

12 Cedar Court, Pasadena CA 94502 · (510) 333-3333
savannahsmith@hotmail.com
Authorized for Post-Secondary Recruitment Direct Hire Authority

OBJECTIVE
CONSUMER SAFETY OFFICER (0696) GS-7

> Add your Post-Secondary Recruitment Direct Hire Authority at the top. Based on this law: https://www.congress.gov/congressional-report/115th-congress/senate-report/205/1

EDUCATION

MAY 2019
BACHELOR OF SCIENCE IN BIOLOGY, SONOMA STATE UNIVERSITY

Achieved the Bachelor of Science in Biology with a concentration of Molecular and Cellular Biology with a minor in Chemistry. Multiyear member of Biology Club and Student Health Advisory Committee. GPA, 3.15 out of 4.0; Dean's List in Spring 2017.

Major Courses:
Molecular Biology, Cellular Biology, & Physiology
Invertebrate Biology
Cellular and Molecular Techniques
Environmental Microbiology & Biotech
Molecular Genetics
Cell Biology
Virology
Independent Research
General Physics Lab I & II

Minor Courses:
Quantitative Analysis
Organic Chemistry I & II
Organic Chemistry Lab I
Metabolic Chemistry

> Add your relevant courses into the resume in the EDUCATION SECTION.

> TRANSCRIPTS: You can upload unoffical transcript into USAJOBS documnets: but if you do get hired, you will probably need to get an Official Transcript sent to the agency Human Resources Office.

JUNE 2012
HIGH SCHOOL DIPLOMA, PASADENA HIGH SCHOOL

> Recent Graduates CAN add awards, honors, AP courses, activities for high school since this is recent experience.

EXPERIENCE

NOVEMBER 2019 TO PRESENT
QUALITY ASSURANCE TECHNICIAN, URBAN REMEDY

Assisting and coaching production members to perform correct SOPs in a Continuous Improvement Environment. Inspecting and releasing cut and washed produce that meets the company's FSQA standard. Measuring pH, specific gravity, and weights of bottled juices for Whole Foods and Urban Remedy. Inspecting and weighing various finished products. Performing allergen tests and ATP swabs during changeover to prevent any allergen and microbial contamination. Recording pH, Brix, and weight data on Microsoft Excel.
40 hrs/week; $22/hr.
Address: 208 S Garrard Blvd, Richmond, CA 94801
Supervisor: Raphael Gomez; (818) 888-8888; may contact.

> Add specific "compliance" details to the resume for Federal Human Resources – hours per week, street address, reference.

Page 2

AUGUST 2018 TO MAY 2019

INDEPENDENT RESEARCH PROJECT, SONOMA STATE UNIVERSITY

Managed research team that develop processes that reduced organics and chemical oxygen demand in brewery wastewater prior to discharge. Routinely collected water and soil samples, analyzed organic removal, and developed lab reports for peer and professor review. Investigated equipment failures and developed alternate solutions. Presented research findings to a panel of judges at the 2019 Sonoma State University's Science Symposium.

15 hrs/week; $500 stipend from Koret Foundation Scholarship.
Address: 1801 E. Cotati Avenue, Rohnert Park, CA 94928
Supervisor: Dr. Michael T. Taylor; may contact.

> CAPSTONE AND INDEPENDENT RESEARCH PROJECTS – Be sure to describe this like a "job" to get credit for this experience and skills.

AUGUST 2014 TO MAY 2019

LABORATORY TEACHING ASSISTANT, SONOMA STATE UNIVERSITY AND CHABOT COMMUNITY COLLEGE

Provided hands on instruction and oversight to lower and upper level students in setup and use of laboratory equipment to include light and fluorescence microscopes, vermifilters, peristaltic pumps, plating, safety procedures, and proper laboratory techniques. Investigated performance and knowledge for compliance of standard operating procedures.

10 hrs/week.
Address: 1801 E. Cotati Avenue, Rohnert Park, CA 94928 & 25555 Hesperian Blvd, Hayward, CA 94545.
Supervisor: Dr. Michael F. Cohen; may contact.

> Add volunteer and unpaid experiences – this is equal to PAID positions. The experience counts, if you create a "job block" for the experience.

SKILLS

Laboratory & Clinical Technical Skills:
- Highly proficient following SOPs, laboratory standards, and performing aseptic techniques.
- Proficient in creating SOPs.
- Highly proficient in micro-pipetting, swabbing, and plating bacteria.
- Highly detail, self-motivating, process orientated, & self-reliant.
- Highly proficient in using a spectrophotometer and performing Chemical Oxygen Demand (COD) analysis.
- Highly proficient in conducting field analyses and measuring physical samples.
- Extensive laboratory experience in isolating, culturing, and analyzing fungal spores and bacteria.
- Highly proficient in performing titrations & measuring pH.

> Add detailed technical and computer skills from your courses, internships, positions.

Computer Skills:
- Highly proficient in Adobe Acrobat Professional, Microsoft Excel, Outlook, PowerPoint, and Word.
- Highly proficient in data analysis on Microsoft Excel.
- Key understanding of Electronic Document Management System (EDMS) and BOX.

Knowledge of Clinical Laws and Regulation:
- Of Good Manufacturing Practices (GMP), Global Food Safety Initiative (GFSI), Internal Organization for Standardization (ISO), National Organic Program (NOP), Hazard Analysis and Critical Point (HACCP) Protocols & Procedures.

> Add specific knowledge of regulations and laws that you have gained from your courses and projects.

REFERENCES

Add here

Know Your Audience: Who Is Going to Read Your Resume?

There are at least two audiences for your resume: the Human Resources (HR) professional and the Selecting Official (i.e., hiring manager).

HR Professional

First, the HR professional will review your resume to determine whether you are qualified for the position. The HR professionals will determine whether your stated qualifications fit the formal requirements of the position and, if so, will classify you as "qualified."

The HR professionals will determine whether your stated qualifications for the formal qualifications for the position, and if so, will classify you as "qualified." Depending on the number of qualified applicants, they usually perform a deeper evaluation to select the "best qualified" candidates. Only the best-qualified candidates are forwarded to the selecting official (your potential supervisor).

Do not assume that the staffing specialist is an expert in your career field, although many are quite knowledgeable. Help the specialist understand and interpret your qualifications by writing your work experience descriptions in language they can understand. If you make the specialist's job easier, you will get more benefit of the doubt. Confuse or obscure your qualifications, and you will earn a lower score than your experience merits.

Selecting Official

The second reader will be the selecting official, who has the discretion in choosing the candidate she or he likes best from the Best Qualified. When the hiring official sees your Federal resume, it is in a folder along with resumes from other highly qualified candidates (your competition). The hiring official does not normally have to interview all highly qualified candidates.

Who gets interviewed? Qualifications are important, of course, but so is the SPARKLE that might be visible in your resume. The SPARKLE could be your accomplishments, volunteer experience, locations where you worked. Is your resume interesting? What stands out? Is there a "likeability factor" in your resume?

How to Find and Use Keywords

Your student Federal resume must include the keywords from the vacancy announcement. Every USAJOBS announcement contains important keywords that you can copy into your resume for a great match to the announcement.

Where to find keywords in a USAJOBS announcement:
1. Specialized Experience requirements in the Qualifications section
2. How You Will Be Evaluated section, which lists additional knowledge, skills, and abilities (KSAs)
3. Self-Assessment Questionnaire

1. Every USAJOBS announcement has a set of different keywords / phrases.
2. Find keywords in the announcement: Duties, KSAs, Specialized Experience, and the Questionnaire.
3. Keywords will become the ALL CAP HEADLINES.
4. Use at least five to seven keyword phrases for your Outline Format resume.

Keywords can also be found in the Position Classification Standards from the Office of Personnel Management.

https://www.opm.gov/policy-data-oversight/classification-qualifications/classifying-general-schedule-positions/#url=0200

OPM.GOV

Matching Keywords to Your Federal Resume, Example #1

Foreign Service Office Management Specialist

DEPARTMENT OF STATE

<u>Department of State - Agency Wide</u>

GS-0343-07, Program Analyst

Qualifications

Specialized Experience

Specialized Experience demonstrates that the applicant has acquired, and is able to apply, a combination of specific knowledge, skills and abilities appropriate to this Foreign Service position.

To qualify as Specialized Experience, the duties must have a combination of secretarial, administrative assistant or office management components of **at least 60% of the work duties**.

Examples of Specialized Experience include, but are not limited to:
1. **Managing calendar(s) and schedule(s)** for one or more senior staff.
2. **Proofing and editing documents**, as well as tracking written materials and maintaining office files.
3. **Preparing documents, handouts, or computer presentations** (e.g. PowerPoint) for meetings, including drafting agendas and following up on commitments made at meetings.
4. **Providing computer support of all types** (e.g., basic and specialized applications, troubleshooting, mobile devices, latest apps, tools and social media) and knowledge management (e.g., developing and maintaining databases, capturing information, and conducting research).
5. **Planning and assisting with official events and visitors**, including tracking budgets and expenses, building and managing guest lists, submitting and monitoring supply requests, tracking guest attendance, and official gifts.

Knowledge, Skills, and Abilities

The applicant's experience, education, and training must show that they have an in-depth knowledge of their field and possess the knowledge, skills and abilities (KSAs) to successfully perform Office Management Specialist duties worldwide.

Best Federal Resume Format

1. **Knowledge of Organizational and Personnel Structures**: Knowledge of organizational hierarchy and structure and the roles and responsibilities of key personnel or offices supporting the organizations goals and objectives, in order to quickly know who to contact for any given issue.

2. **Knowledge of Open Source Research**: Knowledge of key issues within the organization and between the organization and outside entities, including researching information on web sites, social media and/or publications, in order to perform such tasks as examining reports or documents for items of interest to the organization and maintaining files.

3. **Knowledge of Office Computer Programs**: Knowledge at the Microsoft Office Specialist level in Microsoft Office, Word, Excel, and PowerPoint, Access or SharePoint, in order to perform tasks assigned and troubleshoot information technology issues. **NOTE:** Applicants who successfully pass the Oral Assessment **MUST** provide a Microsoft Office Specialist (MOS) Certification in Word 2010 or more recent within 30 days of passing the Oral Assessment (OA). Certifications are obtained from an authorized testing center. Information about Microsoft MOS certification can be found at www.certiport.com. It is the responsibility of the candidate to locate a testing center. All cost incurred in connection with qualifying for this position are the responsibility of the candidate. If the MOS certificate is not received within 30 days of passing the OA, the candidacy will not be continued.

4. **Knowledge of Office Equipment and Troubleshooting**: Knowledge of the use of and ability to troubleshoot standard office equipment including high speed copiers, fax, multi-line telephone systems, cellular or smart phones, tablet or lap top computers and digital senders and scanners.

5. **Cross-Cultural**: Ability to work with people from varied backgrounds, educational levels, and cultural surroundings in order to create and maintain an amiable and success-oriented working environment.

6. **Interpersonal**: Ability to work positively with colleagues in order to promote harmony, cooperation, and good morale.

7. **Decision Making**: Professional judgment and experience to make decisions within appropriate areas of responsibility that move projects forward and enable timely achievement of section goals, including knowing when it is necessary to seek guidance from more experienced employees.

8. **Planning and Organization**: Skill at organizing multiple and varied tasks into an achievable system quickly and accurately with minimal supervision in order to complete duties on time.

9. **Time Management**: Skill in time management and prioritization of work, often under conditions of political unrest and tight deadlines, in order to perform assigned tasks.

10. **Oral and written communication**: Applicants must demonstrate a strong command of the English language to include grammar, spelling and punctuation. Foreign Service Specialist must consistently meet a high standard for English, both written (overall structure as well as grammar, spelling and punctuation) and spoken (overall structure as well as delivery, clarity and succinctness).

Federal Resume Matching State Department Foreign Service Management Specialist

MARK THOMPSON
Address, City, State, Zip
Phone / Email
Authorized for Post-Secondary Recruitment Direct Hire Authority

SUMMARY OF SKILLS
- B.S., Sociology/Criminology and hands-on experience in continuity of operations planning (COOP), emergency response operations.
- Strong research, analysis, problem-solving, and decision-making skills.
- Articulate and effective communicator, orally and in writing.
- Able to achieve results independently and as a member of a team.
- Recognized for initiative, leadership qualities, exceptional work ethic, and strong analytical and critical thinking skills.
- Proficient in Microsoft Word, Excel, and PowerPoint. Conversant in Spanish.

EDUCATION

Bachelor of Science in Sociology – 5/2020
Christopher Newport University (CNU), Newport News, VA – GPA: 3.0/4.0

Relevant Criminology Courses: Criminology, Media and Crime, Social Problems, Research Methods.

Team Projects, Research Papers, and Presentations / Culturally Diverse Research
- Developed social research proposal to study adolescent drug use and the impact of a permissive family or peers on a person's willingness to use drugs. Conducted research to identify published articles on the topic. Designed a survey that could be administered to adolescents.
- Sociological Analysis: On team that analyzed, interpreted, and compared messages in the music of the Muslim and Christian faiths to identify common themes such as praise, worship, forgiveness, and giving thanks.
- Anthropology Team Project: On team that conducted ethnographic research on the Greek Orthodox Church in Newport News, Virginia. Wrote and presented PowerPoint presentation on the beliefs and practices of the culture.

Leadership Activities - Planning and Coordination
- Kappa Kappa PSI, CNU Music Service Fraternity, 2011-Present: Provide assistance to band organizations on campus. Maintained calendar and coordinated logistics for musical performances.
- International Travel, Scheduler, Virginia Ambassadors of Music, 2010: Member of musical group that performed summer concerts throughout Europe,

Best Federal Resume Format

WORK EXPERIENCE

INTERN   01/2014 to 05/2014

Office of Emergency Management, University Police Headquarters   Hours per week: 24
Christopher Newport University
1 University Pl, Newport News, VA 23606
Supervisor: Tammy Smith (777) 777-7777; may contact

Project Assistant for the Update of Disaster Plan: Worked with the Director of Emergency Management to revise CNU's Disaster and Emergency Preparedness Plan. Planned, observed, and participated in emergency preparedness exercises held for citizens. Interfaced with first responders.

Research, Data Analysis: Used a variety of research methods, including in-person and telephone interviews, to gather and compile updated contact information. Edited content to ensure accuracy.

COOP Planning Review: Analyzed and reviewed procedures and guidelines outlined in the Continuity of Operations Plan to gain knowledge and understanding of emergency operations.

INTERN   06/2012 to 08/2012

Office of the Sergeant at Arms (SAA) and Doorkeeper   40 hours per week
U.S. Senate, U.S. Capitol, Washington, DC 20510
Supervisor: John Jones (202) 222-2222; may contact

Managed Special Projects: Supported to the Information Technology (IT) Services Department to set up audio visual and computer equipment for meetings.

Database Management; Document Management: Tracked and managed equipment accountability. Collected, verified, and logged all equipment distributed and returned to the department in the internal log, including smart phones. Maintained accurate paper and electronic files.

Communications: Interfaced and communicated daily with all levels of SAA staff, as well as U.S. Senators and staff, by phone and in person.

Key Accomplishments:

- OFFICE EQUIPMENT CONTROL: Took initiative to label and categorize all new equipment to ensure easy access and accurate inventory control. Successfully completed project that required testing of printers throughout Senate offices to ensure they were operating properly.

Matching Keywords to Your Federal Resume, Example #2

Sample Federal Internship in Health Services

Desired Majors: Epidemiology, Health Services Administration, Public Health, MPH

Posted by: US Dept of Health & Human Services - Substance Abuse and Mental Health Services Administration

SAMHSA's mission is to reduce the impact of substance abuse and mental illness on America's communities. The intern projects will include: working with a diverse group of grantees who serve ethnic minority communities with the highest HIV prevalence rates and populations in this communities who are at risk for or have a substance use or co-occurring substance use and mental disorder. The intern would also support entry into fact sheets and reports; strategic plans and other team strategy planning documents.

Eligibility

The SAMHSA Internship Program is available for students interested and experienced in:

- Public health
- Behavioral and social sciences
- Public policy
- Business communications
- Business administration
- Information technology

Federal Resume Matching SAMHSA Mental Health Internship

SADIE HARRISON
Address, City, State, Zip
Phone / Email
U.S. Citizen
Authorized for Post-Secondary Recruitment Direct Hire Authority

PROFESSIONAL SUMMARY

Bi-Lingual (Fluent in English & Farsi) • Excellent Interpersonal & Communication Skills • Capable Mentor • Skilled Database Manager • Passionate Public Health Advocate Health-Related Research Involvement • 6+ Years Healthcare Experience • Proven Problem-Solver • Proficient at Customer Service

PROFESSIONAL SUMMARY

MASTER OF HEALTH SCIENCES (MHS), Anticipated May 2016
Johns Hopkins University • Baltimore, MD
  –*Major Area of Study:* Mental Health
  –*Certificate:* Mental Health Policy, Economics, and Services
  –*3.43/4.00 GPA*

> MATCH TO YOUR MAJOR / COURSES

RELEVANT COURSEWORK: Statistical Reasoning I & II • Psychopathology • Public Mental Health • Mental Health Services • Epidemiological Inference • Research Ethics • Psychiatric Epidemiology • Public Health Perspectives on Research • Mental Health & the Law • Introduction to the U.S. Healthcare System • Prevention of Mental Disorders • Government in Health Policy • Introduction to Biomedical Sciences

BACHELOR OF ARTS (BA), May 2015
George Washington University • Washington, DC
  –Major Area of Study: Psychology

> MATCH TO YOUR INTERNSHIPS AND JOBS

EXPERIENCE

PATIENT INTAKE COORDINATOR
County Center Dental Group
Supervisor: Dr. Faranak Khasraghi (703-819-7114); May Contact

06/2019 to Present
20 Hours per Week
Woodbridge, VA

CUSTOMER SERVICE: Proactively coordinate with patients and staff to deliver a high-quality customer experience. Effectively communicate with patients to manage the patient intake process. Resolve and follow-up on all customer service issues.

PROBLEM-SOLVING: Research, identify, and resolve ongoing and potential issues negatively impacting customer experience. Propose and implement solutions to enhance office organization, communications, and patient education and awareness.

SOCIAL MEDIA MARKETING: Lead the development and execution of an integrated marketing strategy designed to improve the office's brand recognition.

UNDERGRADUATE RESEARCH ASSISTANT   01/2015 – 05/2015
Men Count (NIH Study) • George Washington University   6 Hours per Week
Supervisor: Jenné Massie (202-994-0603); may contact   Washington, DC

DATA COLLECTION & ANALYSIS: Administered surveys and HIV/STI screenings to collect data for a study conducted by George Washington University and funded by the National Institutes of Health (NIH). Closely analyzed and evaluated survey results and screening data to support researchers in making conclusions for publication.

QUALITY ASSURANCE: Conducted line-by-line reviews of survey results in the research database to identify actual and potential errors. Applied attention to detail while ensuring the quality and efficacy of the study and removing erroneous entries from the database.

INTERPERSONAL COMMUNICATION: Deployed skillful conversation and information sharing to recruit individuals to participate in the Men Count study. Met one-on-one with potential participants at local STD treatment clinics and communicated the purpose of the study, relevant procedures, and provided outreach and awareness information.

Accomplishments:
—During one of my quality assurance reviews, I caught in error in the survey system that could have discredited all of our current survey samples. Because of my thoroughness, the error was identified and resolved, thereby allowing survey re-administration to 700 participants.

—Successfully recruited and enrolled study participants, leading all research assistants in number of participants recruited.

Matching Keywords to Your Federal Resume, Example #3

MATCH TO A SHORT SUMMARY AND YOUR DEGREE / MAJOR

Archives Technician

Qualifications

Specialized Experience: Specialized experience for this position is defined as experience:

-Communicating and responding to inquiries, verbally or in writing;
AND
-Using automated systems to organize and maintain documents;
AND
-Interpreting or applying regulations and policies to accomplish work assignments.

Questionnaire Questions:

3. **Which of the following best describes your experience using records?**
D. I have collected, reviewed, and organized data that I have obtained while using established sources and records from multiple disciplines, databases, and media

6. **From the list below, select the choice that best describes your experience reviewing reports, recognizing errors, and reconciling problems**

8. **Choose the statement that best describes your experience with data retrieval, analysis and reporting.**
A. I have experience obtaining and analyzing disparate information from various systems or data sources in order to prepare an analysis, report or presentation of findings

11. **Which of the following best describes your experience in suggesting improvements in processes and results?**

Federal Resume Matching Archives Technican

ANNE MASTERS
Address, City, State, Zip • Phone / Email
U.S. Citizen
Authorized for Post-Secondary Recruitment Direct Hire Authority

ARCHIVES ASSISTANT / RESEARCH ASSISTANT

Recent college graduate with an M.A. in Applied History and three years of hands-on archival, records management, and historical research experience with federal organizations, historical nonprofits and museums, and private research organizations. Customer-service focused and highly-organized with very strong written, verbal, and interpersonal communication skills. Advanced database/records management, problem-solving, and analytical skills. Proven ability to work independently and on teams.

Archival/Research Expertise includes:

- Arranging, processing, describing and organizing analogue and digital records.
- Writing research aids; digitizing, preserving and maintaining records.
- Providing reference/research services. Managing client consultations for diverse projects.
- Documentary publication, historical editing and exhibits, narratives and exhibit scripts.
- Proficient in use of the National Archives and Records Administration's (NARA) ARC and OPA databases, and the THOMAS database, Library of Congress. Familiar with Archives Tookit.
- **Notable Internships/Projects:** Research Assistant, The Papers of Abraham Lincoln; Archival Intern, U.S. Senator Conrad; and Intern with the Robert E. Lee Memorial Association.

EDUCATION

Master of Arts in Applied History, George Mason University, Fairfax, VA - 5/2019

Specialized Coursework: Administration of Archives and Manuscripts, Study and Writing of History, The Civil War, Clio Wired: An Introduction to History and New Media.

Archivist Practicum: International Teamsters Union, Washington, DC; 3/2018–4/2018; 20 hrs/week
- Communicated and responded to Teamster Union Members regarding document clarification, collecting information and responding to requests for documents. Screened and processed complex union member personnel records. Utilized an automated system, created document categories, scanned and created electronic records. Separated disposable/non-disposable materials. Interpreted Union regulations and policies for management of private personnel information and other documents. Wrote descriptions for finding aid for Teamster Members regarding various inquiries. Created a Fact Sheet for Document Archives. Worked on team with another student and an archivist.

Intern, Buckland Preservation Society, Gainesville, VA; 1/2017–5/2017; 20 hrs/week
- Wrote research paper on the early history of the village of Buckland, VA. Chartered by the Virginia legislature in 1798, Buckland was the first inland town established in Prince William County. It was an important wagon stop on the main east-west road between Alexandria and the territory beyond the Blue Ridge. I researched the history, leaders, early wagon stops. I organized and digitized, for the first time, documents from the beginning of this early US town.
- I also compiled the voting record of Congressman John Love, (1841-1899), Judge and Congressman from Buckland, VA. I organized and digitized important political and Congressional records. Communicated with community leaders concerning research documents, dates and facts. Followed regulations and policies for management of information for the research.

Selected Research Papers: *"Much Chafed by Delay," "The Military Transportation Genius of Jefferson Davis,"* and *"Slavery as a Cause of the Civil War,"* a historiography of slavery.

Office of Personnel Management (OPM) Competencies

Find your core competencies and check them off the list. Add a few of these competencies into the "duties" section of your work experience.

Interpersonal Effectiveness
- ☐ Builds and sustains positive relationships.
- ☐ Handles conflicts and negotiations effectively.
- ☐ Builds and sustains trust and respect.
- ☐ Collaborates and works well with others.
- ☐ Shows sensitivity and compassion for others.
- ☐ Encourages shared decision-making.
- ☐ Recognizes and uses ideas of others.
- ☐ Communicates clearly, both orally and in writing.
- ☐ Listens actively to others.
- ☐ Honors commitments and promises.

Customer Service
- ☐ Understands that customer service is essential to achieving our mission.
- ☐ Understands and meets the needs of internal customers.
- ☐ Manages customer complaints and concerns effectively and promptly.
- ☐ Designs work processes and systems that are responsive to customers.
- ☐ Ensures that daily work and the strategic direction are customer-centered.
- ☐ Uses customer feedback data in planning and providing products and services.
- ☐ Encourages and empowers subordinates to meet or exceed customer needs and expectations.
- ☐ Identifies and rewards behaviors that enhance customer satisfaction.

Flexibility/Adaptability
- ☐ Responds appropriately to new or changing situations.
- ☐ Handles multiple inputs and tasks simultaneously.
- ☐ Seeks and welcomes the ideas of others.
- ☐ Works well with all levels and types of people.
- ☐ Accommodates new situations and realities.
- ☐ Remains calm in high-pressure situations.
- ☐ Makes the most of limited resources.
- ☐ Demonstrates resilience in the face of setbacks.
- ☐ Understands change management.

Creative Thinking

- ☐ Appreciates new ideas and approaches.
- ☐ Thinks and acts innovatively.
- ☐ Looks beyond current reality and the "status quo."
- ☐ Demonstrates willingness to take risks.
- ☐ Challenges assumptions.
- ☐ Solves problems creatively.
- ☐ Demonstrates resourcefulness.
- ☐ Fosters creative thinking in others.
- ☐ Allows and encourages employees to take risks.
- ☐ Identifies opportunities for new projects and acts on them.
- ☐ Rewards risk-taking and non-successes and values what was learned.

Systems Thinking

- ☐ Understands the complexities of the agency and how the "product" is delivered.
- ☐ Appreciates the consequences of specific actions on other parts of the system.
- ☐ Thinks in context.
- ☐ Knows how one's role relates to others in the organization.
- ☐ Demonstrates awareness of the purpose, process, procedures, and outcomes of one's work.
- ☐ Encourages and rewards collaboration.

Organizational Stewardship

- ☐ Demonstrates commitment to people.
- ☐ Empowers and trusts others.
- ☐ Develops leadership skills and opportunities throughout organization.
- ☐ Develops team-based improvement processes.
- ☐ Promotes future-oriented system change.
- ☐ Supports and encourages lifelong learning throughout the organization.
- ☐ Manages physical, fiscal, and human resources to increase the value of products and services.
- ☐ Builds links between individuals and groups in the organization.
- ☐ Integrates organization into the community.
- ☐ Accepts accountability for self, others, and the organization's development.
- ☐ Works to accomplish the organizational business plan.

STEP 07 Apply on USAJOBS

Applying for a Federal job is complex and involves answering a lot of questions, but PERSEVERE and you could land a Federal job!

USAJOBS

Pathways Internship

SUBMIT APPLICATION

Apply on USAJOBS

Applying on USAJOBS involves a two-part process.

Part 1: Get ready on USAJOBS with your profile, resume, and documents.
Part 2: Apply for Federal positions with the Questionnaire and SUBMIT.

The process of applying on USAJOBS can be long and challenging, but applying carefully is CRITICAL to the success of your application. Pay particular attention to these announcement sections:

1. Documents
2. Hiring authorities (who may apply)
3. Education requirements, qualifications, and competencies listed in the announcement (address these in your resume)
4. Questionnaire, if part of the application

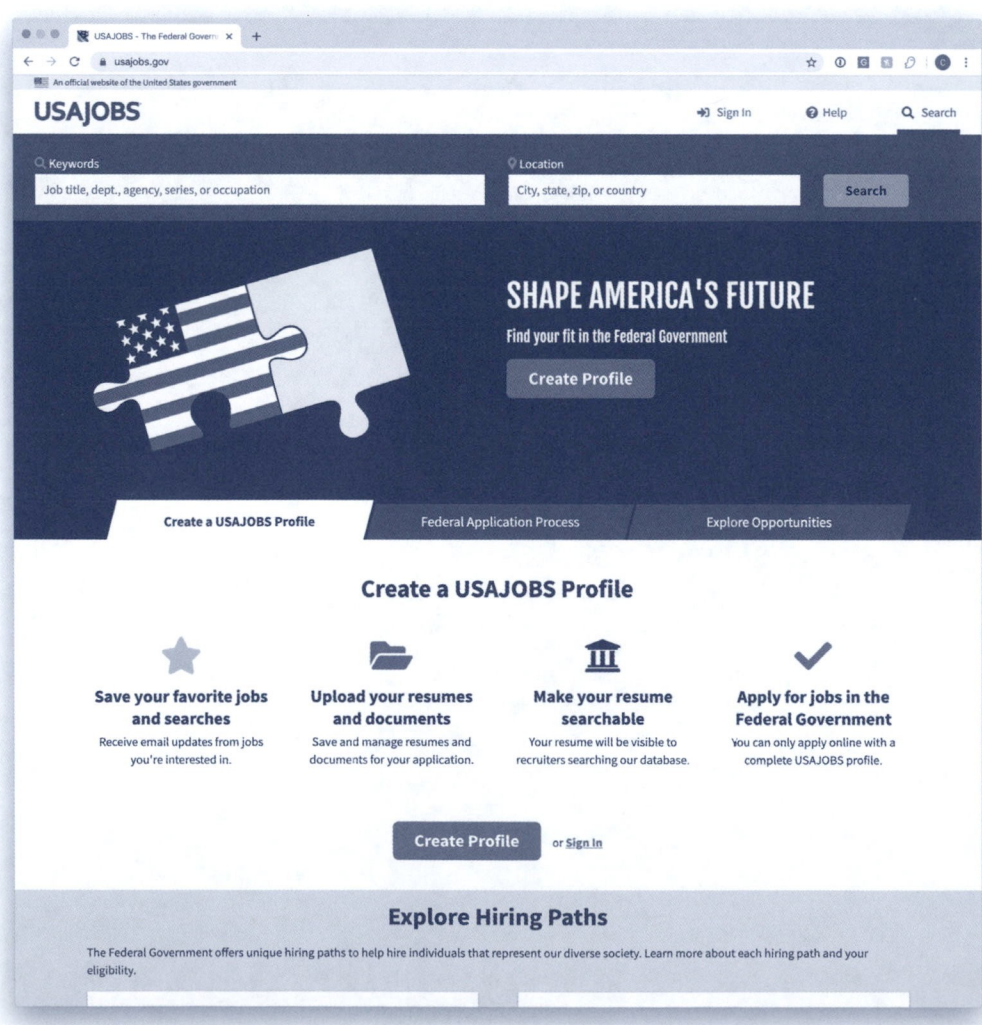

Part One: Get Ready on USAJOBS

Before you begin applying for jobs in USAJOBS, take the time to correctly set up your account and profile. Completing your profile may take at least an hour. To set up the profile, you will need to copy and paste (or upload) your resume; select the types of positions you will accept; select any special hiring authorities that apply to you, such as military or military spouse; and answer other hiring program questions. This critical information is required for you to apply for a Federal position, so complete this task carefully.

Applying for the first time? Use the resume builder to make sure you include all of the required information in your resume. Then download the builder resume from USAJOBS and edit and format the resume for upload. The resume builder does not format the resume and the output is difficult to read. Plus, your resume will be easier to update if it is not in the builder.

STUDENT'S **FEDERAL CAREER GUIDE**

Appointment type & work schedule

What type of work are you willing to accept?

- ☐ All
- ☑ Permanent
- ☑ Temporary
- ☑ Term
- ☑ Detail
- ☑ Seasonal
- ☑ Summer
- ☑ Presidential Management Fellows
- ☑ Recent Graduates
- ☑ Multiple Appointment Types
- ☑ Internships
- ☐ Intermittent
- ☑ Telework

What's the definition of each appointment type?

What type of work schedule are you willing to accept?

- ☐ All
- ☑ Full-Time
- ☑ Part-Time
- ☐ Shift Work
- ☐ Intermittent
- ☐ Job Sharing
- ☐ Multiple Schedules

> Select the types of positions "appointments" and work schedule that you accept.

> Choose your Hiring Paths that you can select. Check this list carefully. Most students and recent graduates will check Open to the Public; Students; and Recent Graduates.

How to choose hiring paths in your profile

The Federal Government offers hiring paths to help hire individuals that represent our diverse society. Agencies use these paths to tell us who they're looking for when they're hiring—whether it's a current federal employee, a veteran, or a recent graduate. There are many different hiring paths including:

- Open to the public
- Federal employees - Competitive service
- Federal employees - Excepted service
- Internal to an agency
- Career transition (CTAP, ICTAP, RPL)
- Family of overseas employees
- Individuals with a disability
- Military spouses
- National Guard & Reserves
- Native American and Alaskan Natives
- Peace Corps & AmeriCorps VISTA
- Senior Executives
- Special Authorities
- Students
- Recent graduates
- Veterans

84

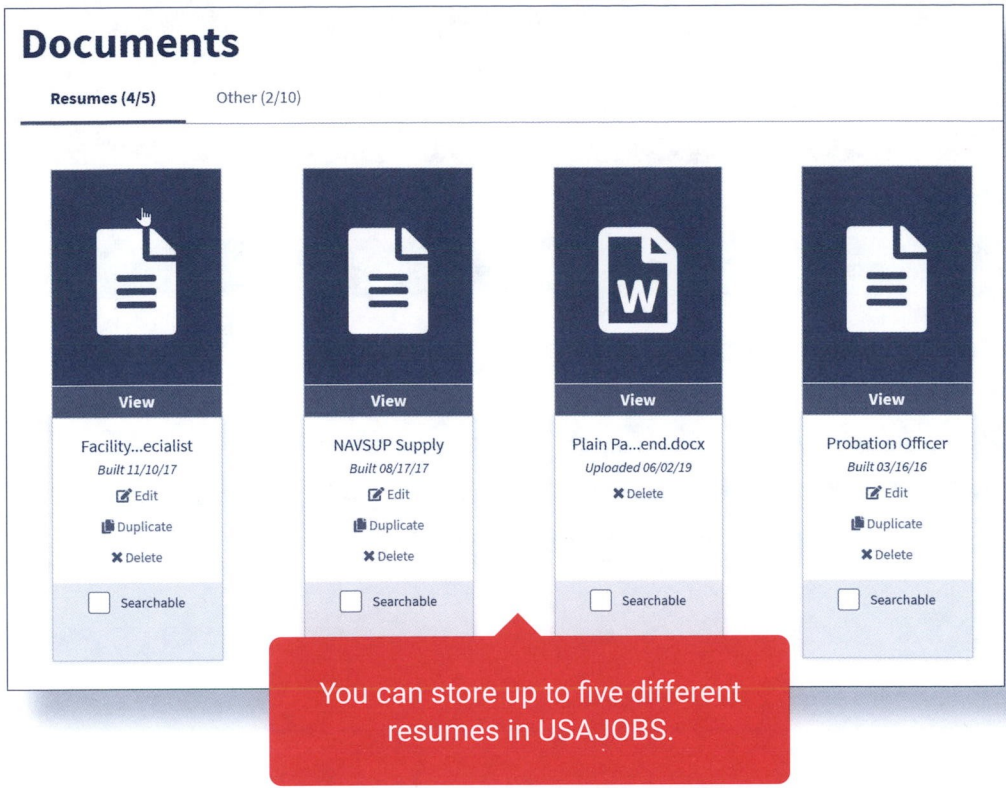

Documents

Resumes (4/5)   Other (2/10)

View

Facility...ecialist
Built 11/10/17
Edit
Duplicate
Delete
☐ Searchable

View

NAVSUP Supply
Built 08/17/17
Edit
Duplicate
Delete
☐ Searchable

View

Plain Pa...end.docx
Uploaded 06/02/19
Delete
☐ Searchable

View

Probation Officer
Built 03/16/16
Edit
Duplicate
Delete
☐ Searchable

You can store up to five different resumes in USAJOBS.

Upload your transcripts as PDFs. If you have multiple transcripts, you can combine them into a single PDF.

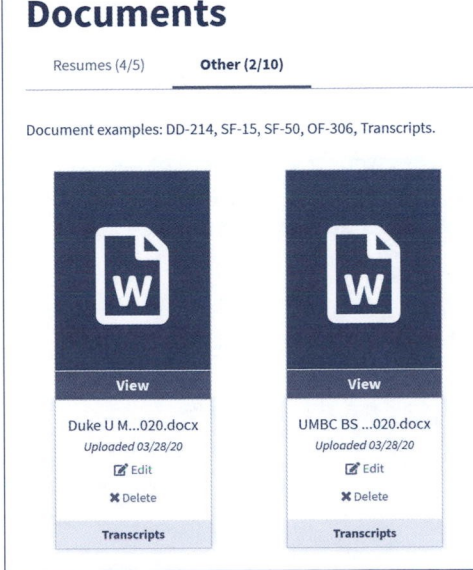

Documents

Resumes (4/5)   **Other (2/10)**

Document examples: DD-214, SF-15, SF-50, OF-306, Transcripts.

View

Duke U M...020.docx
Uploaded 03/28/20
Edit
Delete

Transcripts

View

UMBC BS ...020.docx
Uploaded 03/28/20
Edit
Delete

Transcripts

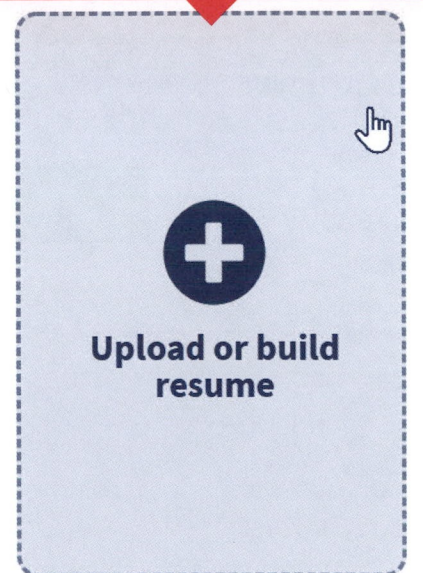

Upload or build resume

> IMPORTANT! Set up SAVED SEARCHES. You can have up to 10 Saved Searches. Sign up to receive daily emails for positions that are of interest to you. Review them and apply quickly. The deadlines are tight!

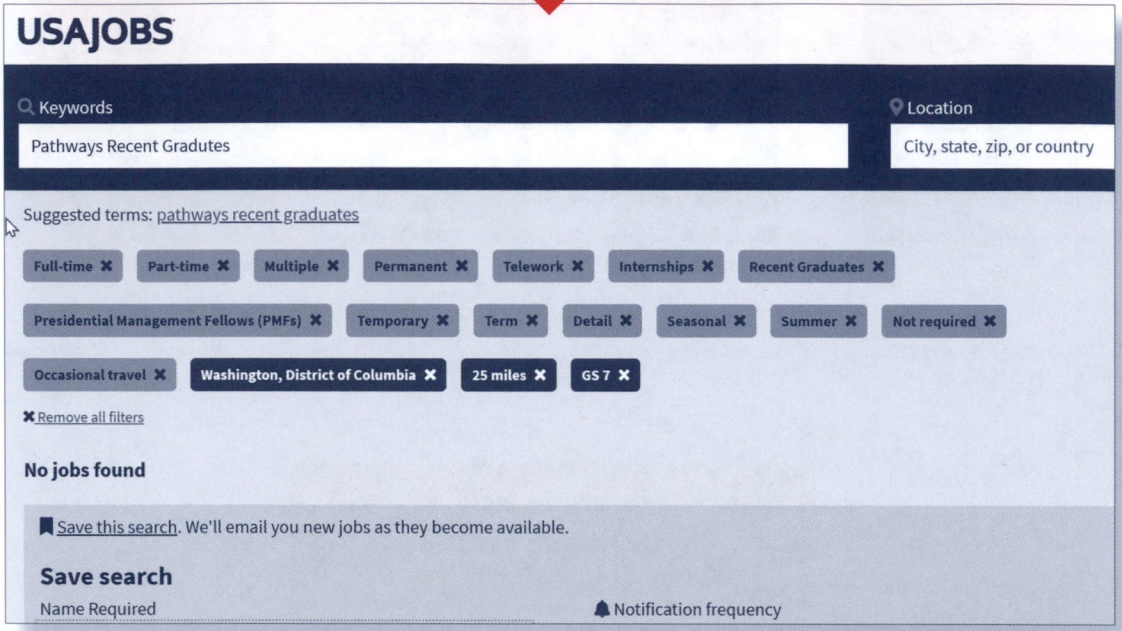

> The dashboard is a very useful page for you to follow while applying for jobs on USAJOBS. You can check the status of the applications that you have submitted; review your saved jobs; and modify your Saved Searches.

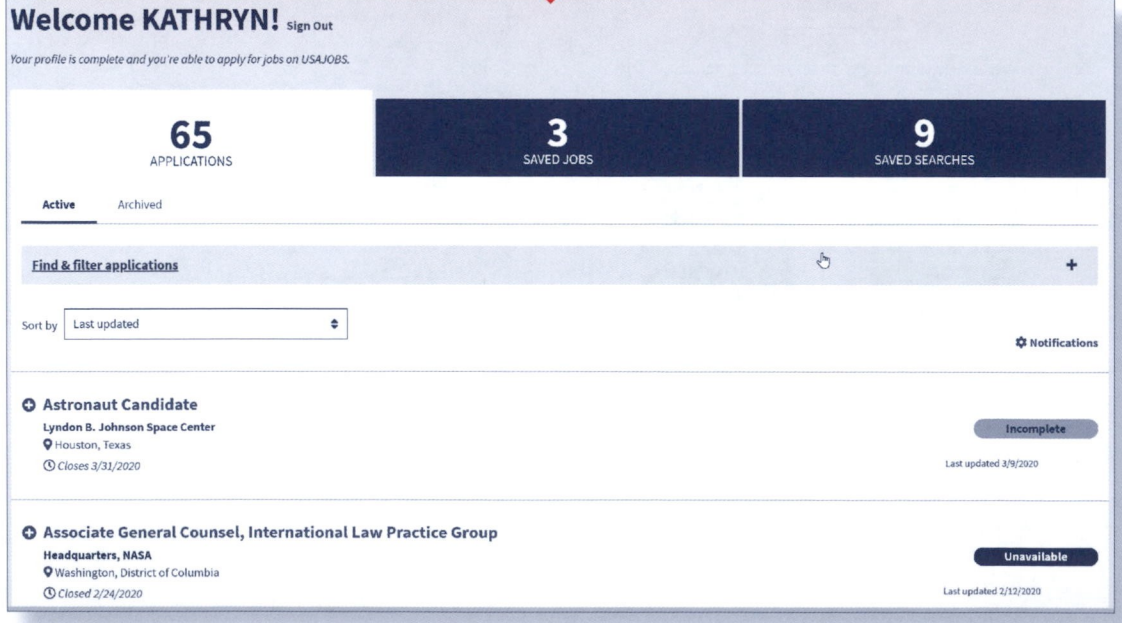

Part Two: Navigate the Questionnaire and Submit Your Application Correctly

Now that Part One of your USAJOBS application is compete, you are ready to begin to actually apply for a position, so complete this task carefully.

Top Tips for Applying for Federal Jobs

1. **Before you actually apply for the position, look for the Preview Questionnaire link in the USAJOBS Announcement:** It can be typically found in the How You Will Be Evaluated, Required Documents, or How to Apply sections. The questionnaire clearly lays out how HR will determine whether or not you are Best Qualified for a position, and this will be your roadmap for determining your application strategy.
2. **Read the questionnaire questions very carefully.** The questions have recently gotten trickier, and you will need to figure out the best answer to each question.
3. **Know that you need to score 90-95% on the questionnaire.** This is a test. If you are unable to achieve a high score, you may reconsider whether or not you are good match for the position.
4. **Do not over or under evaluate yourself.** You should not inflate your answers, but more often, people do not give themselves enough credit.
5. **Review the questionnaire questions against your resume.** Your resume must support your questionnaire answers.
6. **Give yourself at least an hour to actually apply for a Federal job.** Know the deadlines and instructions well ahead of time. Most USAJOBS applications close at 11:59 PM Eastern Time. Try to apply one day ahead if you can, in case there is any problem. If an agency will only accept a specific number of applications for an announcement, apply immediately. Do not wait.
7. **Apply for the Job:** In USAJOBS, when you find an announcement and click on APPLY FOR THE JOB, you will be taken to **another system** for the questionnaire. Usually there are two parts to the Questionnaire: personnel preferences and self-assessment questions.
8. **Job-Related Assessment Questions are very different for each announcement.** Give yourself all the credit that you can with the questions. Think about your courses, papers, projects, non-profit, volunteer, internships, and work experiences to answer the questions and score your skill level.
9. **Review, upload, and move your documents to the second application system.** At the end of the application, you can upload documents, such as a customized cover letter, updated transcripts, or a different resume.
10. **Be sure to hit SUBMIT.**
11. **You can update or change your application until the deadline of the announcement.**

Samples of Job-Related Assessment Questions

1.

Student Trainee (Program Analyst)

DEPARTMENT OF HOUSING AND URBAN DEVELOPMENT

Assistant Secretary for Policy Development and Research

For the GS-07: You must have one year of specialized experience at a level of difficulty and responsibility equivalent to the GS-05 grade level.

14. **Which response(s) describes your experience communicating orally in a professional or academic setting?** Answer to this question is required
   - Responding to inquiries or requests for non-technical information
   - Following-up on written communications from customers
   - Providing information about how to use office machines (e.g., photocopier, phones)
   - Ordering supplies
   - Explaining how to set up a teleconference
   - Contacting others to obtain information
   - Meeting with groups to hear and discuss their concerns
   - None of the above

2.

Student Trainee (Program Assistant)

National Science Foundation

Pay scale & grade: GS 05 - 07
Grade: 06

2. **Which of the following complex type of travel arrangements that you have made? Answer to this question is required. Check all that apply.**
   - Arrange travel for myself on simple routes, such as back and forth to college.
   - Arrange travel for groups of people on simple routes.
   - Arrange travel for myself on multi-city, multi-mode trips, with-in the US, such as going to several locations using at least two of the following modes of transportation – airline, rail, bus, and/or automobile rental.
   - Arrange travel for myself and others on multi-city, multi-mode trips, with-in the US, such as planning and arranging a multi-location family or business trip.
   - Arrange travel for myself on multi-city, multi-mode trips internationally.
   - Arrange travel for myself and others on multi-city, multi-mode trips, internationally.
   - None of the above.

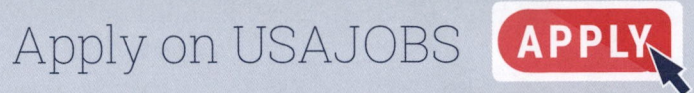

3.

Pathways Recent Graduate, Computer Scientist, GS-1550-07/09/11/12, Census-ABW

DEPARTMENT OF COMMERCE, U.S. Census Bureau

Pay scale & grade: GS 07 - 12
Grade: 07

6. **I have written production-quality code in the following languages: Answer to this question is required**
   - ActionScript
   - CSS
   - HTML
   - Java
   - JavaScript
   - SQL
   - Perl
   - PHP
   - Regular Expressions
   - None of the Above

4.

Pathways Student Trainee (Auditing)

DEPARTMENT OF DEFENSE, Defense Contract Audit Agency

Pay scale & grade: GS 3 – 4
Grade: 03

8. **Apply accounting procedures and practices to financial related duties.**
   - ○ **A.** I do not have experience or demonstrated capability in performing this activity, but I am willing to learn.
   - ○ **B.** I have limited experience in performing this activity. I have had exposure to this activity but would require additional guidance, instruction, or experience to perform it at a satisfactory level.
   - ○ **C.** I have a fair amount of experience and a fair amount of demonstrated capability in performing this activity. I can perform this activity satisfactorily but could benefit from additional guidance, instruction, or experience to perform this activity more effectively.
   - ○ **D.** I have considerable experience and considerable demonstrated capability in performing this activity. I can perform this activity independently and effectively.
   - ○ **E.** I have extensive experience and extensive demonstrated capability in performing this activity. I am considered an expert; I am able to train or assist others; and my work is typically not reviewed by a supervisor. I have received verbal and/or written recognition from others in carrying out this activity.

QUIZ – HOW WOULD YOU ANSWER THESE QUESTIONS?

PATHWAYS INTERNSHIP PROGRAM - STUDENT TRAINEE (CLERICAL/OA)

DEPARTMENT OF DEFENSE, Uniformed Services University of the Health Sciences

Pay scale & grade: GS 3 – 4

5. **From the following responses, please select the statement that most accurately reflects your behavior in demonstrating interpersonal skills.**
   - ○ **A.** I am most likely to ask clarifying questions to better understand when people disagree with my ideas.
   - ○ **B.** I am most likely to actively listen to others when they disagree with my ideas.
   - ○ **C.** I am most likely to disagree with others to defend my ideas.
   - ○ **D.** I am most likely to agree with other ideas that are different than mine.
   - ○ **E.** None of the above.

6. **From the following responses, please select the statement that most accurately reflects your behavior in demonstrating interpersonal skills.**
   - ○ **A.** I seek feedback and constructive criticism from others because it helps me improve.
   - ○ **B.** I am most likely to accept constructive feedback gracefully and will often thank that person for taking the time to give it.
   - ○ **C.** I am most likely to get defensive when others give me constructive feedback.
   - ○ **D.** I am most likely to feel hurt as a result of negative feedback, and have a tendency to withdraw from that person.
   - ○ **E.** None of the above.

7. **This position requires the ability to self-manage. From the following responses, please select the statement that that most accurately reflects your experience in self-management.**
   - ○ **A.** I have set goals and determined how I will evaluate my progress towards those goals. When I accomplish my goals, I like to celebrate reaching that milestone.
   - ○ **B.** I have set goals and compared my current performance as I worked towards those goals.
   - ○ **C.** I have set goals and have worked hard to achieve those goals.
   - ○ **D.** I have set goals, and hope to achieve them someday.
   - ○ **E.** None of the above.

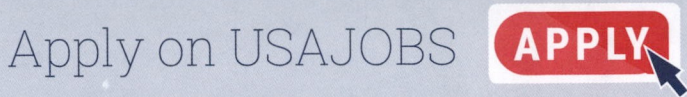
QUIZ – CONTINUED

11. **This position requires the ability to self-manage. From the following responses, please select the statement that that most accurately reflects your experience in self-management.**
    - ○ **A.** I have set goals and determined how I will evaluate my progress towards those goals. When I accomplish my goals, I like to celebrate reaching that milestone.
    - ○ **B.** I have set goals and compared my current performance as I worked towards those goals.
    - ○ **C.** I have set goals and have worked hard to achieve those goals.
    - ○ **D.** I have set goals, and hope to achieve them someday.
    - ○ **E.** None of the above.

12. **This position requires you to complete periods of intern work while completing your academic studies. From the following responses, please select the statement that most accurately reflects your experience in demonstrating self-management skills.**
    - ○ **A.** I have received commendations or awards for my punctuality or attendance.
    - ○ **B.** I am consistently punctual and reliable when I need to be at a specific time and place.
    - ○ **C.** I am tardy or miss expected arrival times less than 10% of the time because I organize my time using a PIM (Personal Information Manager) such as a calendar or personal electronic device.
    - ○ **D.** I am tardy or miss expected arrival times more than 10% of the time.
    - ○ **E.** None of the above.

13. **From the following responses, please select the statement that most accurately reflects your experience in demonstrating oral communication skills.**
    - ○ **A.** I have persuaded uncooperative students to change their role or assignment on a group project.
    - ○ **B.** I have persuaded other students to change the direction and approach on a group project.
    - ○ **C.** I have asked other students questions to resolve problems on a group project.
    - ○ **D.** I have asked other students questions to obtain and clarify information.
    - ○ **E.** None of the above.

14. **From the following responses, please select the statement that is grammatically incorrect.**
    - ○ **A.** I forgot my umbrella today and became sopping wet on my way to work.
    - ○ **B.** Because I forgot my umbrella today, I became sopping wet on my way to work.
    - ○ **C.** Today I forgot my umbrella, on my way to work I became sopping wet.
    - ○ **D.** Having forgotten my umbrella today, I became sopping wet on my way to work.
    - ○ **E.** I forgot my umbrella today; hence, on my way to work I became sopping wet.

STUDENT'S **FEDERAL CAREER GUIDE**

Information Technology Specialist (Customer Support)

DEPARTMENT OF THE ARMY

U.S. Military Academy, Office of the Dean, Department of Physics

Cover Letter Sample
Features Specialized Experience from the Job Announcement

Amanda Smith
Baltimore, Maryland
E-mail: Amanda11@gmail.com
Home Phone: (410) 555-5555

04/04/2020

Recruiter
U.S. Military Academy
West Point, NY

Dear Recruiter,
Please find enclosed my Resume for the position of Information Technology Specialist, GS-2201-7.

My relevant experience for the position includes:

- A **Bachelor's Degree in Information Technology** with a specialization in programming and networking; with an additional 24 credits in virtual learning technology and adult learning.
- I have had numerous experiences **as Teacher's Assistant** and created programming, networking with additional curriculum **for virtual training for college projects,** including Blackboard and Adobe Connect.
- I have demonstrated **patience and skills in working with youth** through my volunteer experiences with soccer and sports for middle school students.

I believe that I would be an asset to your organization because:

- I have **produced adult learning videos with Camtasia** along with PowerPoints to demonstrate study thesis, methods, and results.
- I have skills in **achieving project completion, working under deadlines** and I am result-oriented with my school and internship programs.
- I have **attention to detail,** as evidenced by my projects and internships. I have an **entrepreneurial spirit** for my technology interest and international background.

Sincerely, Amanda Smith
Enclosures: Resume and project list

The Target Position

 The public
U.S. citizens, nationals or those who owe allegiance to the U.S.

Pay scale & grade: GS 5 - 9
1 vacancy in the following location: West Point, New York

Basic Requirement for IT Specialist, GS-07 grade level:
Specialized and Other Experience - One year of specialized experience which includes:
1) Provide basic software training for users;
2) Utilize basic data processing methods in support of the organization's mission;
3) Utilize computer software programs or computer processing programs to prepare reports; and
4) Develop virtual learning technology and curriculum for Physics courses. This definition of specialized experience is typical of work performed at the second lower grade/level position in the federal service (GS-05).

Mandatory Core Competencies for IT Specialist, GS-07 grade level:

The specialized experience must include, or be supplemented by, information technology related experience (paid or unpaid experience and/or completion of specific, intensive training, as appropriate) which demonstrates each of the four competencies, as defined:

(1) Attention to Detail - Is thorough when performing work and conscientious about attending to detail. Examples of IT-related experience demonstrating this competency include: completing work independently that rarely requires editing or review by others

(2) Customer Service - Works with clients and customers (that is, any individuals who use or receive the services or products that your work unit produces, including the general public, individuals who work in the agency, other agencies, or organizations outside the Government) to assess their needs, provide information or assistance, resolve their problems, or satisfy their expectations; knows about available products and services; is committed to providing quality products and services.

(3) Oral Communication - Expresses information (for example, ideas or facts) to individuals or groups effectively, taking into account the audience and nature of the information (for example, technical, sensitive, controversial); makes clear and convincing oral presentations; listens to others, attends to nonverbal cues, and responds appropriately.

(4) Problem Solving - Identifies problems; determines accuracy and relevance of information; uses sound judgment to generate and evaluate alternatives, and to make recommendations.

Track and Follow Up

Here are three actions you can take to track and follow up with your Federal application.

1. Check your application status in USAJOBS.

Welcome KATHRYN! Sign Out

Your profile is complete and you're able to apply for jobs on USAJOBS.

68 APPLICATIONS	**1** SAVED JOB	**9** SAVED SEARCHES

⊕ **Pathways Student Trainee (Auditing)**
Defense Contract Audit Agency
Multiple Locations
⏱ Closes 4/24/2020   Incomplete
                                                                     Last updated 4/11/2020

⊕ **Student Trainee (Passport): Pathways Internship Experience Program (IEP) GS-05 Tucson, AZ**
Department of State - Agency Wide
📍 Tucson, Arizona
⏱ Closes 4/14/2020   Unavailable
                                                                     Last updated 4/11/2020

2. Look for email updates.

From: usastaffingoffice@opm.gov
Date: April 17, 2020 at 11:45:50 AM EDT
To: john.smith@gmail.com
Subject: Notice of Referral Status for Management Analyst (HRSA Global), HRSA-GLOBAL-18
Reply-To: ASKHR@hrsa.gov

Dear John Smith,
Thank you for your interest in the Management Analyst (HRSA Global) position located at the U.S. Department of Health and Human Services.
This notice is a record of your application for Federal employment for the position of a Management Analyst (HRSA Global) at the Health Resources and Services Administration, HRSA-GLOBAL-18-MP.
The following is your referral status for the position or positions to which you applied:

- You have **been referred to the hiring manager for position GS-0343-9**(Global) in Rockville, Maryland
- You have not **been referred to the hiring manager for position GS-0343-11**(Global) in Rockville, Maryland

3. Contact Human Resources Officer listed in the announcement.

Agency contact information

👤 Rockaai Brooks

Phone
615-225-5689

Email
Rockaai.Brooks@va.gov

Address
Robley Rex VA Medical Center
800 Zorn Avenue
Louisville, KY 40206
US

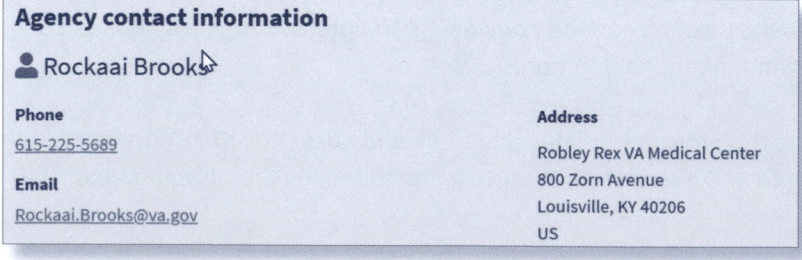

STEP 08 Interview

The Interview for a federal job is a TEST. You need to study the announcement and practice, practice, practice.

08

The Behavior-Based Interview Is a Test

THE FEDERAL JOB INTERVIEW IS A TEST. YOU WILL BE SCORED.

The Federal interview format is called the **behavior-based interview**, which means that they will ask you open-ended questions about your experiences that might be related to the position.

Be prepared to answer 7 to 10 questions that will be situational or experience based. The best answers will be examples that show you already demonstrated the skill or ability in the past. You will want to prepare answers that include accomplishments in the CCAR format (see Step 1). For example, tell how you led a team, provided training for others, or managed a project.

So, for instance, for the IT Specialist position at West Point, the questions could be:

Information Technology Specialist (Customer Support)

DEPARTMENT OF THE ARMY

U.S. Military Academy, Office of the Dean, Department of Physics

Basic Requirement for IT Specialist, GS-07 grade level:
Specialized and Other Experience - One year of specialized experience which includes:
1) Provide <u>basic software training for users</u>; *Can you tell me about a time when you provided basic training for users of a software package?*
2) Utilize <u>basic data processing methods</u> in support of the organization's mission; *Can you tell me about a time when you utilized data processing for your courses or a project? What was the program and what was your project?*
3) Utilize <u>computer software programs</u> or computer processing programs to prepare reports; *Can you tell me about a report you produced, the software you used and the final output?*
4) Develop <u>virtual learning technology</u> and curriculum for Physics courses. *Can you tell me about a virtual learning project and the curriculum you developed or presented in the virtual learning?*

Typical Behavior-Based Interview Questions

Typical interview questions will be:

Job-Related
Open-Ended
Behavior-Based
Skill- and Competency-Based

Competency-Based Sample Interview Questions

Often, an interviewer will ask questions that directly relate to a competency required for the position. Here are some examples.

Attention to Detail: Describe a project you were working on that required attention to detail.

Communication: Describe a time when you had to communicate under difficult circumstances.

Conflict Management: Describe a situation where you found yourself working with someone who didn't like you. How did you handle it?

Continuous Learning: Describe a time when you recognized a problem as an opportunity.

Customer Service: Describe a situation in which you demonstrated an effective customer service skill.

Decisiveness: Tell me about a time when you had to stand up for a decision you made even though it made you unpopular.

Leadership: Describe a time when you demonstrated leadership.

Planning, Organizing, Goal Setting: Describe a time when you had to complete multiple tasks. What method did you use to manage your time?

Presentation: Tell me about a time when you developed a lesson, training, or briefing and presented it to a group.

Problem Solving: Describe a time when you analyzed data to determine multiple solutions to a problem. What steps did you take?

Team Work: Describe a time when you had to deal with a team member who was not pulling his/her weight.

Interview Tips for the Federal Behavior-Based Interview

Steps to prepare and practice

1. Find the job announcement for the interview.
2. Find the SPECIALIZED EXPERIENCE PARAGRAPH to create possible questions for the interview.
3. Write the answers to these questions on paper. For example, you can give an example of a time when you "provide basic training for users of a software package."
4. Write five projects / or assignment "stories" to prepare. Use the CCAR Accomplishment Builder to write your five examples of your past experience (see URL below).
5. Practice speaking your stories with your cell phone or with someone who will listen and give you feedback, such as a career counselor or a friend.

Know the Background
Know the vacancy announcement, agency mission, and office function. Read your resume and KSAs out loud and with enthusiasm.

Do Your Research
Go online to research the agency, department, and position. Read press releases about the organization. Search for recent news about the agency.

Confidence, Knowledge, and Skills
In order to "sell yourself," you need to believe in your abilities. It is not bragging to share what you have accomplished. Don't forget or be afraid to use "I"! Use eye contact.

Types of Interviews
You may be asked to conduct a telephone or in-person interview; it may be with an individual or with a panel or group.

FINALLY: PREPARATION AND PRACTICE ARE KEY TO PASSING THE INTERVIEW.

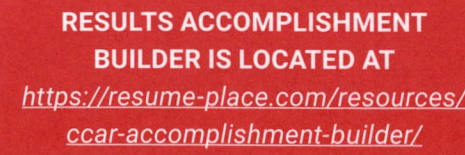

THE CONTEXT-CHALLENGE-ACTION-RESULTS ACCOMPLISHMENT BUILDER IS LOCATED AT
https://resume-place.com/resources/ccar-accomplishment-builder/

Worksheet: Interview Preparation

Start preparing for the interview: answer these questions.

Tell Me About Yourself:
Write a short introduction you could use in an interview. It should include information relevant to the position.

Significant Accomplishment:
Write one significant accomplishment that you will describe in an interview.

Best Competencies:
Make a list of your best competencies.

Most Valuable Skills:
Make a list of your best skills that would be most valued by an employer.

Present your best competencies with a great story or example that demonstrates your real behavior. Use the space below to practice using the CCAR method in answering this question prompt.

Can you give me an example of a problem at work or school that you solved?

★ **CONTEXT**

★ **CHALLENGE**

★ **ACTION**

★ **RESULTS**

SUCCESS STORY

SHAWN'S – TARGET BUDGET ANALYST, GS 7
JOB SEARCH... April 1 to May 15, 2020

I'm still unemployed. That gig in Beale AFB, CA didn't work out. I still have lots of positions that I've been referred, so that's a plus.

Since the Beale Interview, I was also interviewed by Cavalier AFS, ND. (I was getting desperate at that point and applied for the GS-7 job). This base is in the middle of nowhere. They fished my resume out of the reject pile because no one wanted this job.

++++++++++++++++++++++++++++++

I had an interview with Dept of Labor: Bureau of Labor Statistics @ Washington DC, and Dept of Homeland Security: Federal Protective Services @ Kansas City, MO. I liked these two because they're ladder jobs that start at GS-9 and have automatic promotions until GS-12.

++++++++++++++++++++++++++++++++

I just got a tentative job offer. It's the GS-7 budget analyst job @ Cavalier Air Station in North Dakota. I know I should accept it, but it's in the middle of nowhere at starting two steps below I should (with my education). And it only goes to GS-9 after one year. I aim for the GS-12. How much MORE likely is it to get a job transfer to the next highest paygrade when I'm already in the federal pay-system? I should know if I'm going to accept.

+++++++++++++++++++++++++++++

From Shawn,

Kathryn, DOL finally sent a tentative offer for a GS 9! So exciting!
I finished all the required reading and signed everything asked of me already!
I'm so ready to move to DC and start my new life!

+++++++++++++++++++++

LESSONS LEARNED: Follow the lessons in this book and keep applying.

STEP **09** Negotiate Your Job Offer

CONGRATULATIONS! YOU YOU HAVE AN OFFER! WAIT!

Don't accept the offer until you negotiate. Read this step!

Offer Letter

The letter below is an example of an offer letter for a Federal position.

April 18, 2020
Rachel Downing
1000 Event Street
Columbus, OH 20202

Dear Rachel Downing,
Congratulations! You have been tentatively selected for a position as Consumer Safety Officer Reviewer/Investigator (CSO R/I) located in the Division of Food Defense Targeting (DFDT), Office of Enforcement and Import Operations (OEIO), Regulatory Affairs (ORA), Food and Drug Administration (FDA).

The starting salary for this position is set at GS-0696-9 (Step 1, $48,670) per annum, which includes a locality payment of 30.48%. Federal employees ae paid every other Thursday, by direct deposit.

Your Federal benefits include the following: Annual and Sick Leave, Thrift Savings Plan (TSP), yearly cost of living increases, and periodic base pay increases. You are also eligible to participate in: Health, Life, Dental and Vision Insurance; Flexible Spending Account.

To learn more about federal benefits and entitlements, you can visit the following websites:

https://www.opm.gov/healthcare-insurance/healthcare/enrollment/new-federal-employee-enrollment/

https://www.opm.gov/healthcare-insurance/life-insurance/

https://www.benefeds.com/

https://www.opm.gov/healthcare-insurance/flexible-spending-accounts

https://www.chcoc.gov/content/boarding-processes-new-employees-during-covid-19-emergency

This offer will remain tentative until you are able to meet the conditions(s) of employment listed below.

- This position requires the income to consent to criminal history background checks
- This position has a mandatory seasonal influenza vaccination requirement

PLEASE DO NOT LEAVE YOUR JOB OR GIVE NOTICE TO YOUR PRESENT EMPLOYER AT THIS TIME. THIS IS A TEMPORARY OFFER AND CAN BE WITHDRAWN AT ANY TIME PRIOR TO ENTRANCE ON DUTY.

Please reply with your acceptance/declination of this tentative job offer within 2 business days, 5-May-2020. If you are accepting this tentative job offer, please complete the attached OF-306 and return via the SAFE website.

Thank you very much.   Sincerely, HR Recruiter, FDA, Vienna, VA

Superior Qualifications Letter

If you possess superior qualifications for a position that you've been offered, you can negotiate various terms of your offer by writing a letter such as the one shown below. You can try to negotiate one or more of the following: salary (the step within the grade level of hire), recruitment incentives, alternative work location, tuition reimbursement, reasonable accommodations, relocation expenses, and commuter transit subsidy. The justification of superior qualifications needs to be clear and well defined. Request a day or two to respond to the offer, and know that the offer will not be withdrawn if you make a negotiation request.

Rachel Downing
1000 Event Street
Columbus, OH 20202
April 18, 2020

Re: Superior Qualification Statement for Consumer Safety Officer Reviewer/Inspector (GS-0696-9)

Human Resources Recruiter
Food & Drug Administration
Vienna, VA

Dear Human Resources Recruiter:

Thank you for your offer of employment for Consumer Safety Officer with a starting salary of GS-0696-9 (Step 1, $48,670) per annum, which includes locality pay of 30.48%. I look forward to having the opportunity to research and assess risks to meet the Food and Drug Administration's mission at the Division of Food Defense Targeting, Office of Enforcement and Import Operations, Regulatory Affairs.

I believe that my education and experience would contribute immediately to the performance of my duties in researching and assessing risks on imported food/feed to determine if the commodity poses a terrorist threat or significant health risk to the US food/feed supply.

Based on my superior qualifications, I would like to respectfully request that I receive the following in addition to the offered salary and locality pay:

- Starting salary at GS-9 Step 5.
- Federal Student Loan Repayment to provide student loan support (currently in the amount of $75,900).
- Reimbursement of relocation costs, as mentioned in the announcement.
- Telecommuting from home, as indicated in the announcement.

Through my education and work experience, I have had the opportunity to demonstrate superior qualifications in the following ways:

More than 30 hours in biological sciences courses towards a Bachelor of Science in Biology, with a concentration of Molecular and Cellular Biology and a minor in Chemistry:

Major Courses:
Molecular Biology, Cellular Biology, & Physiology
Invertebrate Biology
Cellular and Molecular Techniques
Environmental Microbiology & Biotech

Minor Courses:
Quantitative Analysis
Organic Chemistry I & II
Organic Chemistry Lab I
Metabolic Chemistry

(continued)

Molecular Genetics
Cell Biology
Virology
Independent Research
General Physics Lab I & II

Full-time work experience (three years) ensuring accuracy and reliability with interpreting and evaluating scientific data and drafting reports on technical study findings:

- **Quality Assurance Technician, Urban Remedy (1 year, 40 hours per week).** Created SOPs for Continuous Improvement Environment meeting FSQA standard for Whole Foods and Urban Remedy products.
- **Laboratory Teaching Assistant, Sonoma College (4 years, 20 hours per week).** Trained and directed students in laboratory environment, including laboratory equipment techniques and performing allergen tests and ATP swabs to prevent any allergen and microbial contamination. Recorded pH, Brix, and weight data in Microsoft Excel.

Highly proficient in the following laboratory and clinical technical skills:
- Micro pipetting, swabbing, and plating bacteria
- Using a spectrophotometer and performing Chemical Oxygen Demand (COD) analysis
- Conducting field analyses and measuring physical samples
- Creating and following SOPs, laboratory standards, and performing aseptic techniques
- Isolating, culturing, and analyzing fungal spores and bacteria
- Performing titrations & measuring pH

Demonstrated ability with the following computer skills:
- Adobe Acrobat, Microsoft Excel, Outlook, PowerPoint, and Word
- Data analysis on Microsoft Excel
- Electronic Document Management System (EDMS) and BOX

Possess working knowledge of clinical laws and regulation:
- Good Manufacturing Practices (GMP), Global Food Safety Initiative (GFSI), Internal Organization for Standardization (ISO), National Organic Program (NOP), Hazard Analysis, and Critical Point (HACCP) Protocols & Procedures.

I sincerely appreciate your consideration of this request, and I look forward to beginning a rewarding career with FDA and making an impact within the Office of Division of Food Defense Targeting (DFDT), Office of Enforcement and Import Operations (OEIO), Regulatory Affairs.

Student Loan Repayment Program

GOOD NEWS! You have received your government job offer. Did you know that you can TRY to negotiate the repayment of your Federal Student Loan?

THE LAW

Under 5 U.S.C. 5379 and 5 CFR part 537, agencies are authorized to establish a program under which they may agree to repay certain types of Federally made, insured, or guaranteed student loans as a recruitment or retention incentive for highly qualified personnel.

Excerpt from Federal Student Loan Repayment Program by Office of Personnel Management, 2016

During CY 2016, 34 Federal agencies provided 9,868 employees with a total of more than $71.6 million in student loan repayment benefits. Compared to CY 2015, this represents a 2.7 percent increase in the number of employees receiving student loan repayment benefits and a 3.0 percent increase in agencies' overall financial investment in this particular incentive.

During CY 2016, several Federal agencies utilized student loan repayments to significantly recruit and retain employees in positions related to nursing, science, technology, engineering, and mathematics (STEM). Notably, in CY 2016, the U.S. Department of Defense (DOD) provided student loan repayments to 848 engineers compared to 766 engineers in CY 2015. This amounted to a 10.7 percent increase in the number of DOD engineers receiving student loan repayments.

Closing the skills gap in the STEM workforce is a key component in our efforts to deliver on the core mission of OPM: to recruit and retain a world-class workforce to serve the American people. Employees in STEM career fields are vital to the Federal Government's mission, and OPM is committed to continue working with agencies to help them attract and retain talented professionals using student loan repayments and other human resources management flexibilities.

STUDENT'S FEDERAL CAREER GUIDE

Federal Student Loan Repayments

Agency	Number of Employees Receiving Student Loan Repayments	Percent of Total Recipients	Amount of Benefits Provided	Percent of Total Amount
U.S. Department of Defense	2,857	29.0 %	$22,409,743	31.3 %
U.S. Department of Justice	1,332	13.5 %	$10,304,851	14.4 %
U.S. Department of State	1,256	12.7 %	$10,413,832	14.5 %
U.S. Securities and Exchange Commission	805	8.2 %	$7,285,085	10.2 %
U.S. Department of Veterans' Affairs	711	7.2 %	$4,599,065	6.4 %
U.S. Department of Health and	673	6.8 %	$5,349,207	7.5 %

Human Services				
U.S. Department of Homeland Security	288	2.9%	$2,683,073	3.7%
Subtotal	7,922	80.3 %	$63,044,856	88.0 %
27 Other Agencies	1,946	19.7 %	$8,574,327	12.0%
Total	9,868	100.0 %	$71,619,183	100.0 %

STEP 10

Become a Permanent Federal Employee

It is possible, and sometimes even easy, to become a permanent Federal employee.

Can You Turn a Pathways Position Into a Permanent Federal Position?

To find the answer, simply look at the vacancy announcement for the Pathways position. It will clearly state whether or not you can convert the Pathways position directly into a permanent Federal position. The announcement will also state the requirements you will need to fulfill in order to be considered for a conversion.

Sample Pathways Internship that can be converted into a permanent Federal position:

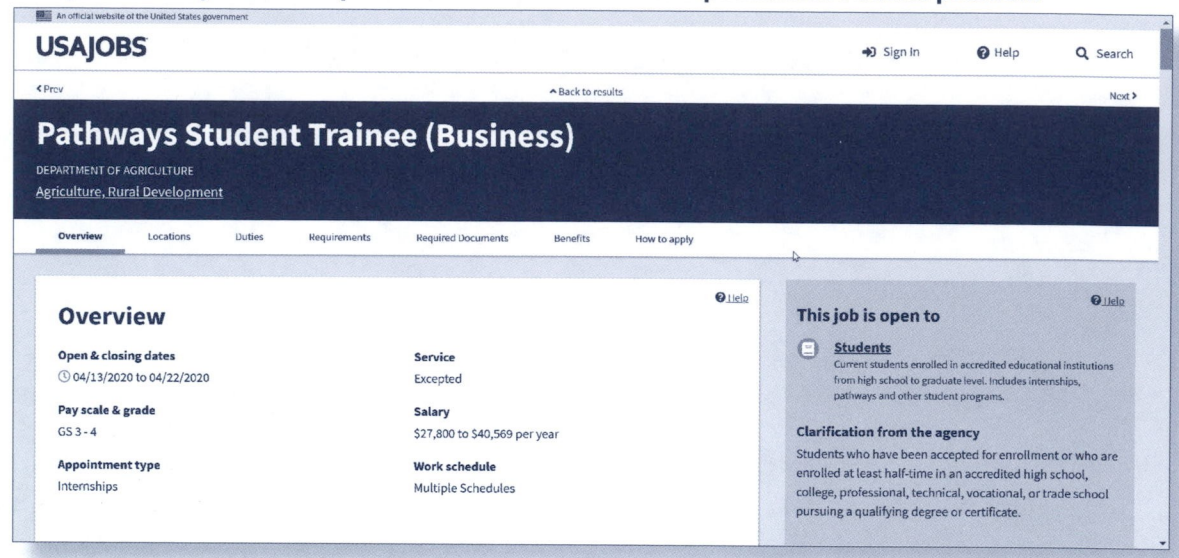

Under "Additional information"

Student Interns must continue to meet the Pathways Program requirements throughout the duration of the appointment. Incumbents will be required to provide proof of continued enrollment and good standing (as Defined by the educational institution), each semester or grading period throughout the internship program. Failure to do so will result in termination of the appointment.

"Upon successful completion of the Pathways Internship Program requirements in accordance with 5 CFR 362.204 (work experience hours, satisfactory performance, educational requirements, mandatory training completion, etc.) you may be non-competitively converted to a term, career¬conditional or career appointment within 120 days".

GOOD NEWS! This Pathways announcement may be converted into a permanent position.

Become a Permanent Federal Employee

Sample Pathways Recent Graduate position that can be converted into a permanent Federal position:

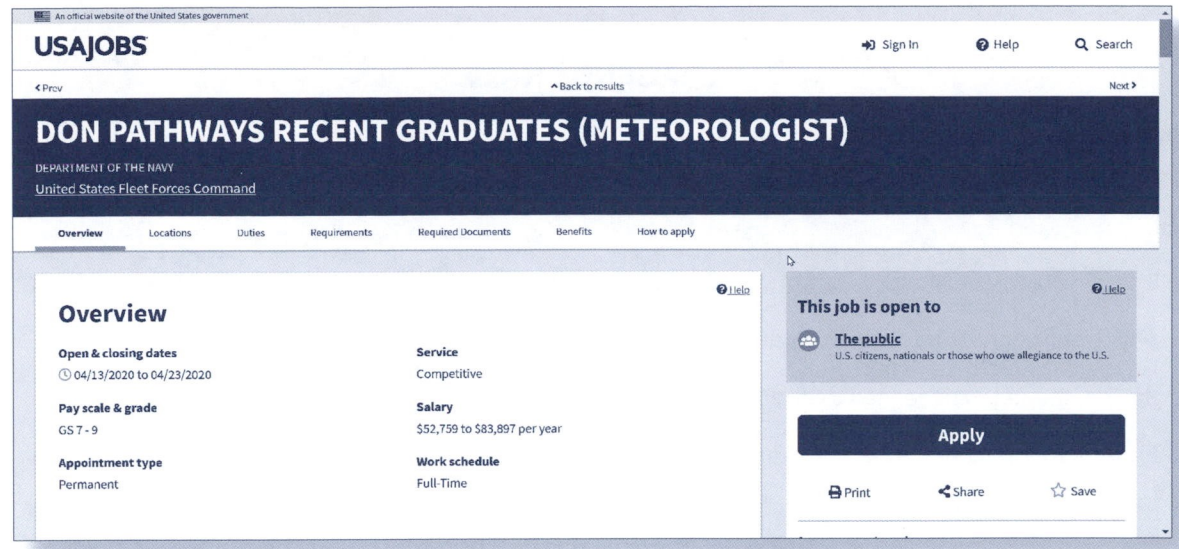

PROGRAM COMPLETION AND CONVERSION:
This vacancy is for a TWO- year program.
[GOOD NEWS:] Recent Graduates may be non-competitively converted to a permanent position in the competitive service (or, in some limited circumstances, to a term position lasting 1-4 years) within 120 days of successful completion of the program.

To be eligible for conversion, Recent Graduates must: Successfully completed at least 1 year of continuous service in addition to all requirements of the program.
Meet the qualification standards for the position to which the Recent Grad will be converted. Meet the qualification standards for the position to which the Intern will be converted Meet agency-specific requirements as specified in the Participant's Agreement and Perform their job successfully

[MORE GOOD NEWS: The Pathways appointment has promotion potential to the GS-12.]
If selected below the full performance level, incumbent may be non-competitively promoted to the next higher grade level after meeting all regulatory requirements, and upon the recommendation of management. Promotion is neither implied nor guaranteed.

If you are in a Pathways position that may be converted into a permanent position, and if you h have determined that you would like to be converted, let your supervisor know that you are interested in converting to a permanent Federal employee.

If the announcement for your Pathways position does not say that you can convert, do the following:
1. Talk with your supervisor about upcoming hiring opportunities
2. Add your Pathways experience to your resume to apply for a permanent Federal position. Use the techniques from this book to help you land a position.

AGENCY NAME
RECENT GRADUATES PROGRAM
Participant Agreement

Appointee's Full Name:	
Appointing Agency/Sub-Agency:	**Pay Scale/Grade Level:** GS-696-7

This is a Recent Graduates Program Participant Agreement between this appointing Agency and the Recent Graduate identified above. The purpose of the Recent Graduates Program is to provide developmental experiences to eligible Recent Graduates with the potential to lead to careers in the Federal Government. The Recent Graduates Program is consistent with guidance contained in the Federal Regulations (5 CFR 362) and this appointing Agency's policies.

Recent Graduate's Roles:	Hiring Official's/ Supervisor's Roles:	Agency's Roles:
★ **Eligibility:** Must be within two years of qualifying educational program completion ★ **Veterans** called to active duty military service following completion of their qualifying educational program will have the remainder of their two-year window to apply when they return, provided no more than six years have passed. ★ Must have an overall GPA of 2.8 on a 4.0 scale or better	★ Create job responsibilities, primarily assignments that contain meaningful development work to target position ★ Prepare for the Recent Graduate's period of employment ★ Identify target position and any promotion potential	★ Fulfill reporting requirements to OPM ★ Administer the application and qualification process ★ Complete a Participant Agreement with each Recent Graduate
★ Successfully complete the Recent Graduates orientation program designed and administered by the hiring Agency	★ Ensure the Recent Graduate successfully completes an orientation program specific to the Recent Graduates Program and participates in the orientation as applicable	★ Create and administer an orientation program specific to the Agency's Recent Graduates
★ Successfully perform the assigned duties listed in his/her position description	★ Provide performance standards and administer performance appraisals consistent with the Agency's appraisal system ★ Deliver it to the Recent Graduate	★ Provide guidance as needed

Appendix A:
Federal Resume Samples

Amita

HIRED! FEDERAL RESUME – 5 PAGES

Auditing, Cyber

Stem Army Cyber Command, GS-2210-9-12

New Graduate, 2018

BS Computer Information, Digital Forensics Information Systems, Auditing, Cyber

AMITA

Springfield, VA 22150
E-mail: amita1@gmail.com
Phone: (666) 666-6666

Citizenship: U.S. Citizen | Security Clearance: Interim Secret

PROFILE

IT Specialist in the Army Knowledge Leader Program, a two-year rotational internship program that provides leadership and technical training in various areas of cybersecurity including securing networks. A CyberCorps Scholarship-for-Service alumni that is serving the country through civilian service to the military. Applying IT knowledge on-the-job acquired from Bachelor of Science, Computer Information Systems degree completed June 2018 at California State Polytechnic University, Pomona, a National Center of Academic Excellence in Information Assurance and Cyber Defense Education.

Possess understanding of **digital forensics**, Linux, **network security**, and **offensive security**. An active learner that is preparing for the CompTIA Security+ certification to continue growing in cybersecurity subject matter expertise to offer to the U.S. ARMY.

Short Profile with keywords and summary of relevant technical qualifications.

CERTIFICATIONS

CompTIA Security+: Studying to obtain the CompTIA Security+ certification by May 2019.

COMPUTER SKILLS

Forensic Analysis: Utilizing DOD-approved software tools including Encase and Forensic Toolkit (FTK) for data acquisition and analysis.

Digital Forensics/Incident Response: WireShark Network and Protocol Analysis

Network Security: Securing networks via software programs including **Cisco Packet Tracer and GNS3.**

Programming: Intermediate Java, Android Application development, Interactive and Responsive Web Development

EXPERIENCE

Certifications and Computer Skills featured.

IT Specialist, Army Knowledge Leader (09/2018-Current)

U.S. ARMY, HQDA CIO-G6

Fort Belvoir, VA 22060

Hours Worked Per Week: 40

Supervisor Name: Mr. John Jones   jjones@army.mil

Okay to Contact Supervisor: Yes

Required information as in the USAJOBS Builder. And short description of the Army Knowledge Leader program.

ARMY KNOWLEDGE LEADER: The Army Knowledge Leader (AKL) program aims to shape tomorrow's cybersecurity professionals through a two-year leadership and technical training. AKL's rotate through various cybersecurity branches to acquire understanding of each area. Upon graduating from the program, an AKL specializes in an area of interest in cybersecurity.

ROTATIONS

IT Auditing (03/04/19 – 06/28/19)

Internship Rotations listed. Extensive hands-on cyber training.

The Army Audit Agency helps to save the Army time and money that can be invested elsewhere in the Warfighter mission.

> **CYBERSECURITY AUDITOR**: Researched the Army Publishing Directorate to locate evidence from documents such as GO 2017-07, AR 25-1, AR 25-2, and AR 10-87 to support audit procedures.

> **POLICY ANALYST**: Conducted draft review of DA PAM 25-2-X, a publication that advises the Army on software assurance. Provided IT insight to senior leadership via a written report.

> **EDITOR**: Delivered constructive feedback to the Army Audit Agency on their writing. Evaluated and edited content to improve writing flow. Ensured that content is objective and final draft is complete. Checked spelling and grammar. Enhanced reader understanding by elaborating on content that may potentially lead to confusion.

KEY ACCOMPLISHMENTS

AUDIT PROCEDURES: Drafted 3 audit procedures in TeamMate, an audit management software system on the following in the Audit of Reciprocity within Risk Management Framework:
1. Roles and responsibilities of stakeholders involved
2. 60 percent In-Process Review findings
3. CIO/G-6 Meeting

KEY ACCOMPLISHMENTS separated from the duties and skills.

WRITTEN COMMUNICATION: Contributed a Cost Savings segment to the *Audit of Reciprocity within Risk Management Framework*. The Army Audit Agency published this work as a part of their joint audit DoD Office of the Inspector General.

Policy, Resources, and Governance (10/2018-01/2019)

The Policy, Resources, and Governance **(PRG)** division of CIO/G-6 develops Army IT policy and enforces compliance to align CIO legal responsibilities.

> **POLICY ANALYST**: Support PRG policy team in maintaining **AR 25-1** and **AR 25-2**, **Army capstone IT regulations**. Review IT-related policy repositories as per Army Publishing Directorate. Collaborate with PRG team on emerging issues in IT Policy such as divestiture of IT legacy financial management systems.

> **CONFIGURATION DATA ANALYST:** Regularly updated documentation of Army regulation status through tools including Microsoft Excel. Provided Weekly Activity Reports that reflected publication status. Monitored the Task Management Tool (TMT) system for any updates.

2

LIAISION: Facilitated communication between PRG team and customer by clarifying project expectations. Collaborated to achieve optimal project outcomes. Demonstrated effective written and oral communication skills.

KEY ACCOMPLISHMENTS
COMMENT ADJUDICATION: Adjudicated 112 comments provided by 48 AWS (Army Wide Staffing) task organizations for the publication, DA PAM 25-1-2, a pamphlet that provides guidance on IT contingency planning for Army organizations. Presented comment adjudication findings to team. As a result, team demonstrated understanding of publication timeline.

INFORMATIVE WRITING/COMMUNICATION: Drafted a SITREP (Situation Report) to keep the CIO informed of the latest PRG updates for CIO/G-6 on the status of **AR 25-1** and **AR 25-2.** This supported Army efforts of furthering policy readiness.

**Engineering Integration, Change, and Asset Management (EICAM) Technical
Intern Northrop Grumman Corporation, El Segundo, CA 90245 (06/2017-08/2017)**
Hours Worked Per Week: 40
Supervisor Name: Mr. John Johns   (333-333-3333) jjohns@aol.com
Okay to Contact Supervisor: Yes

Northrop Grumman, is one of the leading competitors in the aerospace industry and services the government to provide cutting-edge technology. The corporation offers university students summer internships that help students to explore their career interests. Their EICAM Technical Intern program shapes intern skills in areas including Project Management Engineering and Management.

CONFIGURATION DATA ANALYST: Reported information to manage configuration item documentation including proposed change status and compared these with technical baseline. Accounted for configuration status with the help of software tools including Enovia, a product lifecycle management software tool, and GRANTA, an engineering material item database.

CONFIGURATION VERIFIER AND AUDITOR: Audited process flow of Engineering Change Proposals for Advanced Extremely High Frequency (AEHF) Satellite program. Communicated audit findings to team enabling them to identify gaps in process flow. Briefed audit conclusions during team meeting.

LIAISION: Facilitated communication between customer and vendor when relaying information on Engineering Cost Estimates. Shared updates to configuration items with team and customers. Bridged the communication gap between customers and team.

KEY ACCOMPLISHMENTS

TECHNICAL DOCUMENT WRITING: Drafted letters to multiple vendors to obtain Engineering Cost Estimates for HIPing an aluminum specimen, a process that entails using high pressure and temperature to densify an aluminum specimen in efforts of removing any metallic porosity. These letters specified desired temperatures and pressures that customer desired. Coming from a non-engineering background, the task was to familiarize oneself with the technical terminology. The end of this project, I had become acquainted with the HIPing process and language through communication with vendors.

TEAM PLAYER/PUBLIC SPEAKING: Participated in an intern team to create an educational poster informing Northrop Grumman audience and public on the importance of Ground Based Strategic Deterrence (GBSD) initiatives. Presented on the Intercontinental Ballistic Missile (ICBM) at an Engineering Forum at the Northrop Grumman, El Segundo location.

Instructional Technology Assistant, eLearning
California State Polytechnic University, Pomona, CA 91768 (02/2017-05/2017)
Hours Worked Per Week: 20
Supervisor Name: Mr. John Johns (333-333-3333)
Okay to Contact Supervisor: Yes

TECHNICAL SUPPORT: Resolved and followed up with help desk tickets from customers within 24 hours timeframe. Guided professors to navigate technically complex learning technologies. Provided remote technical support to instructors that were not available on campus via the Adobe Connect software, a video and screen sharing collaboration tool.

EDUCATOR: To supplement technical support, delivered instructions to instructors using learning tools. Provided follow-up materials for instructors to review after coaching session. Increased content quota of Blackboard courses as requested by instructors to promote student learning outcomes.

KEY ACCOMPLISHMENTS

LEARNING CONSULTING: The Director of eLearning needed suggestions to increase the rate that students read prior to attending class. Leveraged prior tutoring experience to advise on success strategies. Proposed solutions including in-class extra credit quizzes, interactive games, and classroom reading discussions to enrich reading. Discussed rationale behind students not reading prior to classes and how to make reading more enjoyable. After the consulting session, Director of eLearning decided to implement these strategies in her future classes to increase the rate of students reading.

PUBLIC SPEAKING: Presented to groups of 15-20 technology-driven individuals on Clipix, an online organizational tool. Demonstrated application to encourage use. Motivated 12 faculty members to incorporate this application to improve their teaching career.

4

EDUCATION

California State Polytechnic University, Pomona, CA (09/2016-06/2018)
College of Business, Bachelor of Science, Computer Information Systems   GPA: 3.80

- Information Assurance Track, Magna Cum Laude honors distinction, June 2018
- CyberCorps: Scholarship-for-Service Program, September 2017-June 2018
- Dean's List, California State Polytechnic University, Pomona, September 2016-June 2018
- President's List, California State Polytechnic University, Pomona, May 2018

> Education is AFTER the Army Cyber Internship. The Internship is more important now!

Relevant coursework: Systems Development Project, **Digital Forensics**, Network Security, **Information Systems Auditing**, **Internet Security**, Intermediate Java Programming, Management Information Systems, Interactive and Responsive Web Development, Database Design and Development, Systems Analysis and Design, and Business Telecommunications

ACADEMIC PROJECTS

> Academic projects are still here. They will disappear after 2 or 3 more years!

DATA ANALYTICS PROJECT MANAGER (03/2018-05/2018): To help shape the planning and organizing of the Social Innovation Lab at Cal Poly Pomona, distributed a campus-wide survey to over 23,717 students to assess lab user needs. Analyzed the survey data of over 300 students using Qualtrics, a software tool that helps enterprises make informed decisions. Attracted 60 students to sign up to use the lab resources. Created charts and graphs to illustrate breakdown of student interests. Met with clients on a weekly basis to answer questions. Supervised Qualtrics training of customers prior to project termination.

ASP.NET WEB PAGE DEVELOPMENT (11/2017-12/2017): In an Interactive and Responsive Web Development course, created a dynamic web page for bike riders to post reviews of their favorite hiking trails. ASP.NET, a Microsoft developed web application framework, was applied to enable interaction between the review writer and the web page. Presented this web page and explained the ASP.NET framework to a class of 30 students. Received an "A" grade for this project.

QUANTUM CRYPTOGRAPHY (08/2017-10/2017): Performed a review of the literature on quantum cryptography. Created an educational poster to provide visual at a Cal Poly Pomona Cybersecurity Awareness event, an event that aimed to increase the information assurance knowledge of non-technical undergraduate and graduate students. Outcome: Achieved third place out of 50 students for best poster presentation and awarded $130.00 in cash prize.

DATABASE DEVELOPMENT (03/2017-06/2017): Simulated database development for Pine Valley Furniture, a hypothetical company presented during a class case study. Through the software tool **SQL Server 2014**, developed a database and executed queries. Presented deliverables including entity-relationship diagram and formulated queries.

Shawn

HIRED! FEDERAL RESUME – 3 PAGES

Target Budget Analyst, Financial Analyst, GS-0560-9
MBA, Business and Logistics, Accounting, Managerial Finance

SHAWN B.
Address Line 1 • Address Line 2
Phone # • Email Address
U.S. Air Force Veteran, 30% or More Disabled

> Add your Veterans' Preference at the top.

EDUCATION

MASTER OF BUSINESS ADMINISTRATION (2019)
Embry-Riddle Aeronautical University • Daytona Beach, FL
GPA: 3.9/4.0 • Delta Mu Delta Honors Society in Business
  – *Business and Logistics Coursework:* Accounting for Decision Making; Managerial Finance; Organizational Behavior; Venture Creation; Aviation/Aerospace Systems Analysis; Advanced Aviation Economics; Strategic Marketing Management in Aviation; Supply Chain Management; Airline Operations & Management; Lean Six Sigma; Operations Research

> Add your relevant courses in the resume.

BACHELOR OF SCIENCE IN AVIATION MAINTENANCE (2017)
Embry-Riddle Aeronautical University • Daytona Beach, FL
GPA: 3.2/4.0 • Minors in Business Administration & Avionics Line Maintenance
  – *Business and Logistics Coursework:* Marketing; Financial Accounting; Human Resource Management; Corporate Finance; Microeconomics; Business Law, Social Responsibility and Ethics in Management; Advanced Computer Based Systems; Business Information Systems; Aviation Labor Relations; Aviation Technical Operations; Logistics Management

> Add your GPA over 3.0.

UNIVERSITY PROJECTS

OPERATIONS & FINANCIAL RESEARCH
Alaska Airlines

> Course / business projects demonstrate professional skills in Finance and Budget!

1/2019 – 4/201

LOGISTICS & FINANCIAL ANALYSIS: Studied and analyzed the Alaska Airlines' business model, financial strategy, network structure, schedule, and fleet. Explored the feasibility of 3 potential routes that could be added to the network and used the Sabre database to evaluate the competition and related feeding markets.

BUDGET & PROFITABILITY PROJECTIONS: Applied data to *Greg's itinerary choice model* to calculate profitability of proposed routes in relation to budget projections and the airline's financial expectations. Discovered that 2 of the proposed routes were profitable and presented a report.

LEAN SIX SIGMA FINANCIAL ANALYSIS
AMI Aviation Services, LLC

> Skills in Budget and Analysis are demonstrated here.

1/2019 – 4/2019

BUDGET & PERSONNEL MANAGEMENT: Analyzed and proposed lean changes within formal budget constraints; worked with a team of students and AMI management to lean the work environment within the limitations of a leased space while adhering to fire codes.

PROGRAM IMPROVEMENT: Built the model for a feasible second shift to optimize and prioritize the workflow of aircraft harnesses that demand hundreds of man-hours to build, thereby making the time-to-product both quicker and more financially efficient.

STRATEGIC MARKETING MANAGEMENT   8/2018 – 12/2018
Payment and Competitor Analysis for Blaise, LLC

FINANCIAL STREAMLINING: Worked with a team of students to analyze the payment methods of current major airlines, including the air carriers reward systems and credit card partner. Researched alternative payment options and the extension of instant installment credit to the airline travel marketplace. Researched the one financial tech firm offering the service and partnering with the firm.

EMPLOYMENT

MANAGER   4/2007 – 5/2015
Kabuki Sushi Bar & Restaurant   Small business, budget, accounting,   **40 Hours per Week**
Centreville, OH 45458   management skills demonstrated.
Supervisor: Bob Brown (123-456-7891)   Add hours per week.

FINANCE, ACCOUNTING & BUDGET MANAGEMENT: Responsible for budgeting, cost control, payroll, and basic book-keeping. Planned menus, estimated food and beverage costs, and purchased inventory. Completed restaurant opening and closing procedures, balanced cash till, and managed cash deposits to the company's bank account. Evaluated inventory for food and alcohol, scheduled replenishment stock for low supply. Monitored sales of each item and revised order schedules to reflect demand.

SUPERVISORY EXPERIENCE & PERSONNEL ADMINISTRATION: Supervised, scheduled, and motivated more than 20 staff members. Assigned work schedules and assessed performance. Oversaw training programs for staff to enhance customer experience and increase profit through suggestive up-selling.

ORAL & WRITTEN COMMUNICATION: Investigated and resolved food/beverage quality and service complaints, ensuring customer satisfaction and repeat business. Developed and delivered substantive reports to owners on potential marketing and financial strategies to improve profitability.

FINANCIAL SYSTEMS EXPERTISE: Used financial and logistics software to schedule deliveries of food to the restaurant and to justify expenditures within the budget planning model for the company. Utilized an order-by-text system to schedule next-day deliveries from other distributors such as Gordon Food Services, Ocean Providence, True World, Chicago Food Corp, and Pepsi.

FREELANCE CARTOONIST   4/ 2007 – 5/2015
Self-Employed   Entrepreneurship, innovation, creativity   **20 Hours per Week**
Centreville, OH   and small business management.

FINANCIAL MANAGEMENT: Coordinated payments, project budgets, and administered all aspects of a freelance business operation. Applied financial knowledge to work with clients to ensure projects remained within budget while also leveraging my expertise to ensure profitability for the effort.

EFFECTIVE COMMUNICATION: Able to collaborate and communicate with clients to identify requirements and clarify details of art projects. Starting at the planning phase of the project, involved clients in every following step of the illustration process.

MILITARY HISTORY

SENIOR AIRMAN
US Air Force
Ellsworth AFB, SD 57706

USAF Parts - accountability, automation, justifying expenditures!

12/2002 – 4/2007
40 Hours per Week

FINANCIAL & RESOURCE ACCOUNTABILITY: Responsible for ordering parts through the Air Force's Core Automated Maintenance System (CAMS) and justifying all expenditures based on financial models and requirements. Maintained accountability on serially-controlled parts to ensure necessary cost-savings.

PROGRAM OVERSIGHT & COORDINATION: Conducted B-1B ground engine run for maintenance, in-flight troubleshooting, and engine change. Conferred with other specialist sections to discuss corrective actions, and assisted in the maintenance of related aircraft systems, including hydraulics, environmental and electrical. Troubleshot and remedied aircraft problem while on the tarmac during emergency red-ball maintenance, saving the aircrew from having to move to another aircraft.

VOLUNTEER EXPERIENCE

CLUB FOUNDER & OFFICER (P.A.W.S.)

Non-profit management, leadership, and financial management.

1/2017 – 12/2019

LEADERSHIP: Co-founded club that monitors and cares for the colony of working cats at Embry-Riddle University. Served as Colony Manager and then Vice President. Led club meetings briefing members of news within the club, volunteer opportunities, and coordinating with the trapping teams.

ORGANIZATIONAL & BUDGET MANAGEMENT: Completed all necessary paperwork for establishing a new club including by-laws, club leadership structure, mission-statement, task procedure, income statements, budgets, and emergency medical protocols.

CERTIFICATIONS

OFFICE SPECIALIST: EXCEL 2016, Microsoft Corp.
CERTIFIED BLOCKCHAIN EXPERT (#12316813), Blockchain Council
CS-PRO FUNDAMENTALS CERTIFICATION, SCM Principles, issued by Council of Supply Chain Management Professionals (CSCMP)
LEAN SIX SIGMA YELLOW BELT, American Society for Quality
PROFESSIONAL DEVELOPMENT CERTIFICATE OF ACHEIVEMENT, Emergency Management Institute
DEGREE OF MERIT, National Speech and Debate Association

MEDALS & HONORS

Good Conduct Medal
Global War on Terrorism Expeditionary Medal
Global War on Terrorism Service Medal
National Defense Service Medal

Jeremy Denton

HIRED!

INTELLIGENCE ANALYST, GS-0132-9/12
Department of Homeland Security
US Marine Corps, E-5
BA, Government and Public Policy

JEREMY D. DENTON

1234 Anywhere Street
City, State, Zipcode
Phone: 555.555.5555
Email: jeremy.d.denton@gmail.com

OBJECTIVE: Career Ladder Position, Pathways Program, Management Analyst, Intelligence Analyst, Security Specialist

PROFESSIONAL EXPERIENCE:

- Substantial leadership and planning experience as Helicopter Crew Chief in USMC.
- Skilled in critical thinking, analysis and data management.
- Outstanding record of achievement as Pilot with 16 Air Medals.
- US Marine Corps, 08/2003 to 01/2008, honorable discharge
- Security Clearance: Secret (active), Interim Top Secret (active)

EDUCATION:

Bachelor of Arts, Government and Public Policy, *cum laude*. University of Baltimore, Maryland. GPA: 3.7 out of 4.0; January 2020.

- DRAFTED MAJOR PAPER ON LEGAL NORMS: Successfully drafted and submitted a paper exploring the organization, function and processes of law making institutions in the American justice system. The paper also analyzed legal ethics and their role in major cases over a five-year period.

- LED TEAM PROJECT ON GOVERNANCE: Coordinated research and writing efforts of 2 other students on a major governance project. Reviewed fundamental theories of governance, researched literature on related topics, and drafted a recommendation-focused paper on "best practices" in public administration.
- CO-PRESENTED PAPER AT MAJOR CONFERENCE: Participated in a panel presentation at the national Conference on Ethics and Social Justice. Delivered prepared commentary on ethical challenges in government leadership, through the lenses of disparity, power and privilege.

International Marine Transportation, New York Maritime College, Bronx, NY, 35 credits, 09/2012-05/2013.

PROFESSIONAL EXPERIENCE

01/2019 to present, **INTELLIGENCE ANALYST**; E-5; Maryland National Guard (Reserves), Baltimore, MD,

- DATABASE ADMINISTRATOR: Maintain, process, and manage security clearance database and associated procedures for 1-175th Infantry Battalion utilizing JPA. Initiate clearance process for personnel requiring new clearances, and identify personnel whose authorization has been revoked. Process and secure sensitive and/or derogatory personnel information in close coordination with Army security managers. Enter coded information into Army systems.

- TRAINING: Lead numerous classes on Army critical skills and required knowledge, including Operational Security and Human Trafficking.

- SAFEGUARDING PERSONAL INFORMATION: Protect file integrity of 600+ individual files, each containing sensitive personal information.

- OPERATION PLANNING: Help plan real world training exercises for upcoming peacekeeping deployment to the Sinai Peninsula in support of 1979 Camp David Accords.

KEY ACCOMPLISHMENTS:
- SELECTED TO BE BATALLION ELECTRONIC WARFARE NON-COMMISSIONED OFFICER: Outstanding work ethic led to selection as the Battalion Electronic Warfare NCO. As EWO, trained to use the electromagnetic spectrum to deny the enemy's ability to attack US and Allied personnel with remote devices. Work directly with commanders to ensure the proper utilization of Electronic Warfare to safeguard friendly personnel.

10/2014-01/2018, **HELICOPTER CREW CHIEF**; E-5, Sgt, 3rd Marine Air Wing, Marine Corps Air Station Miramar, San Diego, CA

- TEAM LEAD / FLIGHT CREW MEMBER: Planned, organized, led, and performed maintenance on CH-53E Super Stallion helicopters. Supported more than 2,000 sorties in several major exercises.

- SCHEDULING AND COORDINATION: Performed daily inspections on assigned aircraft; assisted in preflight inspections performing final checks; monitored aircraft performance during flight; assisted as a lookout and advised pilot of obstacles and other aircraft.

- CRITICAL THINKING AND PROBLEM SOLVING: Analyzed weight, mission, cargo and prepared aircraft for maximum defense. Utilized evaluative and technical skills in operating aircraft mounted weapons systems.

- PLAN AND ORGANIZE WORK: Assisted in the supervision and administration of aircraft maintenance operations. Developed methods and procedures to improve efficiency of the Flight Crew, especially in flight operations or emergency maintenance procedures.

KEY ACCOMPLISHMENTS:
- LOGGED 1,200+ FLIGHT HOURS WITHOUT A SINGLE LOSS OF LIFE OR AIRCRAFT during two tours in Iraq and in the United States, including during combat conditions, armed interdictions, border patrolling, and medical evacuations of military and civilians.

- AS CAPTAIN, performed essential systems and safety checks for every aircraft under my care daily prior to operations (up to 14 helicopters). Led team effort in achieving a perfect safety record for my unit over 3.5 years and two combat tours.

MILITARY TRAINING

    Naval Aviation Air Crewman Candidate School at NATTC, NAS Pensacola, FL.
    Survival, Evasion, Resistance, and Escape (SERE) School at Brunswick, ME.
    "A" and "C" school, CH-53E Crew Chief Training Syllabus
    Plane Captain (PC) Ground syllabus for type aircraft.

AWARDS AND RECOGNITION

    Navy/USMC Achievement Medal, 2017
    2 Iraq Campaign Medals
    16 Air Medals
    USMC Good Conduct Medal, 2016
    Global War on Terrorism Service Medal, 2014
    National Defense Service Medal, 2013
    Sea Service Deployment Ribbon
    Expert Rifle Badge and Expert Pistol Badge (2d Award)

OTHER INFORMATION:

    Maryland Drivers License; Current Interim Top Secret Government clearance
    Eagle Scout, Boy Scouts of America; CPR and First Aid Certified through the Red Cross

Greg Martinez

HIRED! COMPETITIVE STUDENT FEDERAL RESUME – 3 PAGES

IT Specialist, Cyber, IA, GS 2210-7

BS, Computer Science; Minors: Statistics and Economics

GREG MARTINEZ

5552 November Lane, Silver Spring, MD 20906
Mobile: (240) 123-4567
Email: GMartinez18@gmail.com

Direct Hire Authority - Post-Secondary Students

> Add: Direct Hire Authority

> Optional: Add intro paragraph

PROFILE

University of Maryland Baltimore County (UMBC) College Senior seeking career-focused position maximizing an academic degree in Computer Science and the real-life experience gained through multiple internships and part-time employment. Selected for a highly competitive ORISE Fellowship with the U.S. Department of Energy (2017-2018). Experienced with agile design methodologies, including the design/development of database applications. Participant in multiple hackathon and cyber challenge events, gaining experience with multiple cyber security applications and tools. Seeking internship opportunities for the Summer 2018 as well as permanent employment following a December 2018 graduation date.

EDUCATION

University of Maryland Baltimore County (UMBC), Baltimore, MD 21250. Completed 151 semester hours in a BS degree program in Computer Science (Minor: Statistics and Economics). (GPA: 3.17/4.0). Expected graduation: December 2018. *Relevant coursework*:

Computer Science: Computer Science I for Majors, Discrete Structures, Social/Ethical Issues in IT, Computer Organization & Assembly Language, Principles of Programming Languages, Data Structures, Computer Architecture, Principles of Operating Systems, Software Engineering I, Database Management Systems, Artificial Intelligence

Economics: Principles of Microeconomics, Principles of Macroeconomics, Intermediate Microeconomic Analysis, Intermediate Macroeconomic Analysis, Benefit-Cost Evaluation, Economics of Natural Resources, Health Economics

Statistics: Introduction to Statistics, Probability & Statistics for Science and Engineering, Time Series Data Analysis, Introduction to Probability Theory, Applied Statistics

> List Courses, add credit hours, if the announcement is asking for specific credits.

COMPUTER SKILLS

Platforms: Microsoft Windows Desktop (7/8/10), RedHat Linux, CentOS
Development: C++/C, Python, Java, JavaScript, Kotlin, ARM assembly, Git, Node.js
Applications: VirtualBox, R, QuickBooks, SAS Enterprise, SharePoint, Veeam Endpoint Backup, Ninite, Microsoft InfoPath
Document Management: SharePoint
Database/Web: Oracle, SQL, MySQL, Amazon Web Hosting (AWS)
Office Products: Microsoft Office, Visio, Google Docs

> Add technical, software skills for all resumes.

Add course project descriptions to demonstrate experience and skills.

ACADEMIC PROJECTS

- **Academic Coding Project** – *Building Linux Shell in C,* 250 Lines of Code (LOC) (CMSC421/ Principles of Operating Systems): Designed a shell for Linux that supports a few basic features of a full-fledge *nix shell. The shell presents the user with a command prompt; accepts a command input of an arbitrary length; parses command-line arguments from the user's input; and passes them to the user-defined program. The application was not allowed to use any external libraries other than the system's C library (2018).

- **Academic Database Project/Presentation** – MySQL Database/Application (CMSC461/Database Management Systems): Completed a team project and presentation for a database application supporting a hypothetical rental agreement application. Designed a MySQL database from an entity-relationship model and a corresponding relational schema for use with a web application supporting SQL queries for selecting, adding, and dropping data. Briefed the design in an oral classroom presentation (2017).

- **Academic Coding Project/Presentation** – *Sin/Cos/Tan ARM Project*, 150 LOC) (CMSC411/ Computer Architecture): Completed a team project to design and develop an ARM assembly program that calculates $\cos(x)$, $\sin(x)$, and $\tan(x)$ using the CORDIC algorithm to calculate trigonometric functions. Briefed the development challenges and final design during an oral classroom presentation (2017).

INTERNSHIPS/FELLOWSHIPS

ORISE Fellow (11/2017 – Present)
U.S. DEPARTMENT OF ENERGY
19901 Germantown Road, Germantown, MD 20874
Part-Time: 16 hours/week
Base Salary: $18.00/hour
Supervisor: Nancy Dement, (202) 123-4567; *May contact*

Add compliance info, plus OUTLINE FORMAT with KEYWORDS. And be specific with projects and duties.

TECHNICAL PROCESS DEVELOPMENT: Selected for a 6-month (11/2017 – 05/2018) ORISE Fellowship supporting the U.S. Department of Energy. The Oak Ridge Institute for Science and Education (ORISE) Program offers internships, fellowships, and research experiences for students pursuing science, technology, engineering, and math (STEM) disciplines. As an ORISE Fellow, complete multiple assigned projects to design and implement SharePoint-based technical and administrative workflows supporting DOE mission. Capture workflow information through interview and documentation review; develop workflow diagrams to capture the proposed workflow; and implement the end-to-end workflow in the SharePoint installation. Employ Microsoft Infopath to design and distribute electronic forms used within the workflow. Develop and present documentation on the proposed workflows.

Design Intern (07/2016 – 08/2016)
SPANISH SATELLITE TELEVISION
3440 Willis Blvd., Los Angeles, CA 90010
Full-Time: 40+ hours/week
Base Salary: Unpaid
Supervisor: Jean Hollis, (626) 111-2222; *May contact*

JOURNALISM RESEARCH/ANALYSIS: Completed a 2-month internship with Spanish Satellite Television, a Spanish-language television broadcaster that services 160M+ Spanish-speaking viewers. Completed research projects to develop background for articles on U.S.-related topics for the corporate InfoNews Channel. Used web and other database resources to compile and analyze statistics on assigned topics. Developed comprehensive research papers used for the development of broadcast journalistic articles.

Accomplishments: Assigned projects included a statistical analysis of minority enrollment at the United States Military Academy (USMA) and Virginia Military Institute (VMI) and U.S. participation and viewpoints on the 2016 Rio de Janeiro Olympics. The internship included an introduction to the corporate broadcast journalism processes.

JOB EXPERIENCE

IT Consultant (09/2017 – Present)
ROUTE 144 CLASSIFIED
P.O. Box 21275, Baltimore, MD 21228
Part-Time: 10 hours/week
Base Salary: $15.00/hour

Supervisor: Darryl Phillips, (410) 111-2222; *May contact*

> Salary and supervisors / phone is optional. Add if it would be helpful to your application.

DATA ANALYSIS Complete data analysis and market research studies pertinent to the publication needs of a local classified advertising publication. Compile pertinent employment, sales, and other customer-centric metrics and develop Excel pivot tables to highlight trends and produce business forecasts with the goal to increase sales.

CUSTOMER SERVICE: Assist with customer support functions for training customers. Use QuickBooks to receive and post training advertising orders. Manage the advertisement ordering process, from order receipt to publication. Validate and reconcile advertising sales invoices.

IT Consultant/Tutor (07/2014 – 08/2016) *(Summer Job)*
STUDENT HOST INTERNATIONAL, LLC.
101 Penny Brook Drive, Newark, DE 19711
Full-Time: 40+ hours/week *(Also Part-Time; 5 hours/week; 08/2016 – 05/2017)*
Base Salary: $14.50/hour
Supervisor: Jack Simms, (302) 123-4567; *May contact*

ACADEMIC TUTORING/MENTORSHIP: Served as a tutor and mentor for international high school students preparing for U.S. academic and internship programs. Assisted with academic instruction in mathematics and oral and written English. During the academic year, provided part-time tutoring via Skype.

Accomplishments: (IT Consulting): Completed the setup and configuration of Windows-based desktop systems for use by the Student Host summer program. Installed, configured, tested, and troubleshot 10 new Windows-based desktop systems. Restored legacy personal computers to usable condition. Ensured the compliance of each desktop system with a standard, secure Windows configuration. Implemented an automated system backup capability using Veeam Endpoint Backup. Managed the automated batch installation of system software, layered products, apps, and utilities using the Ninite package management system.

> Describe accomplishments and special projects separate from the overall duties.

Volunteer and outside activities do demonstrate competencies and skills.

VOLUNTEER/EXTRACURRICULAR EXPERIENCE

UMBC Cyber Dawgs: Participant in the weekly UMBC Cyber Dogs non-credit program, which provides hands-on experience with a broad range of cyber security applications and tools. The weekly program includes a one-hour lecture followed by a lab-based, hands-on project. Example projects completed during the 2017-2018 academic year included:

- Configuring CentOS as an all-in-one server for DNS and SSH, using a Public-Private key pair, MySQL, and Git.

- Configuring Linux iptables to implement state checks, HTTP/HTTPS, incoming/outgoing SSH, mailing protocols, and name resolution.

- Configuring a Virtual Machine (VM) to serve Domain Name Service (DNS BIND), SSH, MySQL, and Git (Gogs).

- Exploring the iptables firewall configuration utility in Linux, including forwarding with pre/post routing, writing policy chains, and using other useful commands and flags.

Hack UMBC: Participated in the October 2017 Hackathon sponsored by Hack UMBC. Working in a 3-person team, completed a coding challenge within the 24-hour period established by the event, which had the theme to design a product with a positive social outcome using Application Programming Interfaces (APIs) from the McCormick spice company and Spotify, a music, podcast, and video streaming service. Used Amazon Alexa, Amazon Web Hosting (AWS), Node.js, and Javascript to interface with the APIs to produce a product entitled "Rap me a Recipe", which provided a playlist of rap music soundbites based on descriptions of recipes.

Hackital: Participant in the 32-hour, November 2017 Hackital hackathon in Washington, D.C. Working in a 3-person team, created a Chrome plugin that uses Google Natural Language and Facebook Graph APIs to filter Facebook feed posts and comments based on a "toxicity" score.

LANGUAGES

English: Fluent
Spanish: Fluent

Language skills are critical in culturally-diverse government organizations.

ANNE CRANE

HIRED – FIRST APPLICATION SUBMITTED!
Health Insurance Specialist, GS-11/12
Center for Medicare & Medicaid Services
1 Year of PhD studies in Counseling Psychology
MS, Applied Psychology
BA, English Literature

Anne Crane
1136 Canton Avenue
Baltimore, MD 21230
Phone: 240-444-4444
Email:anne.crane@gmail.com

Job Number: HHS-CMS-DE/MP-12-77777
Position: Health Insurance Specialist (GS-0107)
Grade: GS 09-12

Objective: To obtain a position in healthcare

> Feature the keywords from the announcement.

Summary of Skills:

Statistical Analysis
Data entry and analysis using SPSS, SAS, and Excel;
Data visualization techniques (graphs, charts, scatterplots, structural equation modeling);
Matrix/Linear Algebra methods;
ANOVA, MANOVA, Correlation, Linear Regression, Multiple Regression, Chi Square, Chronbach's Alpha, post hoc assessments, and various other methodologies;
Moderating and mediating variables

Research Analysis
Planning and design of research studies on social media, women's healthcare, and healthcare training; budget design and analysis; facilitating data collection and administration of assessment tools; analysis of findings and interpretation of results; presentation of results at conferences; powerpoint presentations and research paper publications

Healthcare
Provided mental healthcare to elementary and middle school children and their families in Baltimore City; provided families on Medicaid information and resourcesfor affordable healthcare; research presentation on healthcare and harmful

practices towards women in Nigeria; created proposal for college mental health outreach program targeting Asia Americans and international students; assisted retirees on transitioning to Medicare from university healthcare benefits; helped navigate Baltimore City families, while working as counselor in inner city school, to affordable healthcare services and discussed utilizing Medicaid

Computer Skills:

SPSS, SAS, Peopleware Pro, Oculus, RefWorks, Opus, Global Link
Word, Adobe-Acrobat, Excel, Access, PowerPoint, Pagemaker

Education:

1 year of PhD studies in Counseling Psychology
September 2011-May 2012
University of Pennsylvania, Philadelphia, PA
Overall GPA: 3.91/4.0

> Software skills are listed close to the top.

M.S. in Applied Psychology, 2011
University of Baltimore, Baltimore, MD
Overall GPA: 3.87/4.0

B.A. in English Literature,2007
University of Towson, Towson, MD
Overall GPA: 3.54/4.0

Honors:

Cum Laude, Psy Chi (National Psychology Honor Society), Dean's List

Related Coursework:

> List relevant courses.

Intermediate Statistics, Univariate Statistics, Multivariate Statistics, Research Methods I and II, Professional Writing and Communication, Ethics and Law, Law and Society, Human Development, Multicultural Counseling, Tests and Assessments, Human Development Across the Lifespan, Biological Basis of Behavior (Neuropschology), Psychopathology and Diagnosis, Psychological Development, Adolescent Development

Major Papers and Research:

> Major research papers and projects are detailed.

Crane, A., CWSI, Walters, T., Lieberman, A., Trenton, S., & Siu, L. (2012). Harmful Practices: Violence Against Women in Nigeria. Paper to be presented at symposium at the 30th International Congress of Psychology. 1st author and member of team creating presentation for international conference. Collaborated with Nigerian NGO in order to present their data on violence against women and proposed legislation. Created powerpoint for presentation and prepped teammates for presentation in South

Africa in July, 2012. Interpreted the data and determined that findings suggest harmful practices such as female genital mutilation are still in existence in Nigeria. Findings also show that the government although these practices exist, members of the community as well as governmental officials are reluctant to discuss the issue.

Crane, A. Preston, C., & Frame, S. (2011). Individuals' Impressions: the Effect of Gossip and Gender on Personality Disorders. Poster presented at 23rd Annual Association for Psychological Science Convention (May 2011). Designed and administered study on human behavior, gossip, and social media. Created methodology for study and created assessment tool. Administered assessment tool to subjects. Gathered consent from subjects and university, in the form of consent forms and IRB. Used 2-way ANOVA to analyze data in SPSS. Found that female subjects were more likely to view females poorly due to negative gossip, rather than males. Presented findings at Association of Psychological Science annual conference in Washington, DC (July 2011).

Did you design a project?

Healthcare Article Critques. Evaluated and critiqued 3 current journal articles on healthcare relating to Asian Americans, multicultural competency, and the effect of racial matching on the patient's perception of quality care. Wrote papers regarding critique of the articles' methodology, sampling method, and assessments. Presented critiques to class (November 2011).

Self-Care Brochure: Designed brochure for healthcare professionals on the importance of self-care. Presented coping strategies such as, meditation, deep breathing, and counseling (December 2011).

University Suicide Prevention Program: Created proposal and design of a suicide prevention program. Outreach focused on Asian Americans students and other minorities. Designed program in terms of outreach procedures, workshops, and presentations. Outreach including clubs on campus, sports teams, Greek life, and incoming freshman. Workshops included role-playing, information on additional services, and warning signs. Presented proposal to university students (October 2011).

Presentation on the Millon Clinical Multiaxial Inventory III assessment tool (May 2012). Discussed evolution of the assessment tool. Evaluated assessment tool and created visual aid of pros and cons. Found that although the Millon has high validity, it has an issue with response bias. Assessed which populations the Millon is appropriate for.

STUDENT'S FEDERAL CAREER GUIDE

129

Work Experience:

> Month and year is mandatory. Salary is optional. Hours per week: mandatory.

Benefits Assistant (contracted employee)　　　　　**September 2012 – Present**
Johns Hopkins University
1101 E 3rd St., Baltimore, MD 21218　　　　　　　　*$16.50/hour*
Supervisor: Craig Raine　　　　　　　　　　　　　　*40 Hours/Week*
　Duties: Worked with retirees and current employees to help them submit necessary paperwork and information for healthcare benefits. Assisted retirees on their transition from JHU health insurance to Medicare/Medicaid.

Graduate and Research Assistant　　　　　　　　**September 2011 – May 2012**
Lehigh University
111 Research Drive, Bethlehem, PA 18015　　　　　*$7,500 stipend*
Supervisor: Dr. Carlotta Regent　　　　　　　　　　*20 Hours/Week*
　Duties: Conducted literature reviews and organized articles for future research using RefWorks. Collected and analyzed previous relevant research for a proposal of funding on a study about women graduate students in healthcare professions. Evaluated proposed research studies for technical feasibility and methodology. Edited and prepared articles and book chapters for publications. Analyzed statistical data using SPSS and created tables and graphs. Researched assessment tools for current studies. Worked in collaboration with a team on researching and analyzing previous relevant research findings, including implications, issues, and future directions.

Research Assistant　　　　　　　　　　　　　　**September 2010 – May 2011**
University of Baltimore
1420 N. Charles Street, Baltimore, MD 21201　　　*Not paid*
Supervisor: Dr. Barnard Wilth　　　　　　　　　　*15 Hours/Week*
　Duties: Conducted literature reviews and researched articles for proposal of research study regarding mental healthcare required due to the protean career. Analyzed previous relevant research and results. Assisted with conducting studies on the impact of careers on mental health. Collected and entered data in SPSS. Facilitated collection of data and administration of tests and assessment tools. Researched assessment tools and measures for future study. Analyzed various factors such as, time needed, price of assessment tools, and labor to create budget for future research study.

Psychology Extern September　　　　　　　　　　　**2010 – May 2011**
University of Maryland School Mental Health Program
701 W. Pratt St., 4th FL, Baltimore, MD 21201　　*Not paid*
Supervisor: Moses Muhammed, MSW　　　　　　　　*20 Hours/Week*
　Duties: Worked as a mental health therapist in a Baltimore City public Elementary/ Middle
　School. Administered intakes to potential clients. Provided confidential individual and group counseling to clients and families on Medicaid and Medicare. Evaluated students and provided DSM diagnoses. Assisted families in finding appropriate healthcare options

Philip Sang

HIRED!

Mechanical Engineer, GS-0830-9/12
U.S. Army Corps of Engineers

Masters in Aerospace Engineering

BS, Aerospace Engineering

BS, Mechanical Engineering

PHILIP W. SANG

111 Kahula Street • Honolulu, HI 96822

Mobile: 808-333-3333 • Email: psang11@gmail.com

GOAL: To utilize my education and passion for engineering disciplines and problem-solving to contribute to a team effort in planning and carrying out assignments.

LICENSURE AND CERTIFICATION

Engineering License Certification: Engineer-In Training: Mechanical Engineering, 10/2010, State of California

COMPUTER PROFICIENCIES: Applications: Microsoft Office, AutoCAD 2010, Pro/Engineer, MathCAD, CAD/CAM with Numerical Control; Programming Languages: C++, MATlab 2010a

EDUCATION:

MASTER OF SCIENCE IN AEROSPACE ENGINEERING   08/2017-12/2019

University of Southern California (USC), Los Angeles, CA 90089

GPA: 3.33, 24 Total Semester Credits

Developed and honed skills in all phases of engineering projects. As part of teams and individually, designed, researched and developed solutions to engineering problems. Made engineering calculations, wrote specifications and selected and identified materials. Conducted testing and troubleshooting to assure design met needs. Observed, tracked and evaluated performance data and prepared reports on findings. Made recommendations for best designs, testing, operations and maintenance.

ACADEMIC DESIGN PROJECTS:

- Next Generation Mobile Cloud Computing Technology: Member of team that designed device that could be used for mobile cloud computing; device had stronger processing power than a cell phone, but was more portable than a laptop. The project consisted of modifying and compromising between various available technologies to produce a design that would be functional, reliable and economical. Design consisted of cell phone that projected a laser keyboard onto any flat surface with glasses to serve as a visual display and gloves to interact with objects on the visual display; the entire system remotely connected to a desktop at home with strong computing power.

- Dynamics of a Rotating Baseball: Lead programmer and numerical analysis assistant for five-person team that calculated the aerodynamic forces placed on a rotating baseball as it travels from the pitcher to the batter. Location of fastball pitch was determined, which determined the initial velocities and angles at which the pitch was thrown. Used MATlab code to simulate the movement of a different pitch with a different spin with the same initial angles.

- COURSEWORK: Dynamics of Incompressible Fluids, Engineering Analytical Methods, Engineering Analysis, Compressible Gas Dynamics, Advanced Mechanical Design, Project Controls- Planning and Scheduling, Systems Architecting, Combustion Chemistry and Physics, Principles of Combustion, Advanced Dynamics

BACHELOR OF SCIENCE, AEROSPACE ENGINEERING   06/2017
BACHELOR OF SCIENCE, MECHANICAL ENGINEERING
Illinois Institute of Technology (IIT), Chicago, IL 60616
GPA: 3.56 out of 4.00, 128 Total Semester Credits
Supervisor: Candace Worth, Ph.D., Phone: 312-333-3333, May contact

Graduated Cum Laude, 05/2010

ACADEMIC DESIGN PROJECTS:

- Smoke Wire Flow Visualization Over Car Models: Team leader for project to determine which car design reduced aerodynamic drag the most. Took pictures of streamlines exposed by oil on a heat wire producing smoke trails in the airflow of a wind tunnel. Photos showed which car models experienced flow separation or the extent of the flow separation, the leading cause of aerodynamic drag. Then used photos to determine which car design was best suited for the tested wind speeds.

- Large-Scale Building Solar Air Conditioning System: As member of six-person team, served as lead for system design and CAD design, and numerical analysis assistant. Researched and designed solar-powered air-conditioning system. The final design used parabolic mirrors that would focus the sun's rays to one point, heating up the molten salt that is then stored in a large silo, capable of holding enough energy to power the system overnight. The salt would heat liquid ammonia into a gas that runs through a heat exchanger with air, which cools the air during summer. During winter, the heat exchanger would run in reverse to warm the facility. The thermodynamic equations were placed into an energy equation solver that solved the unknown parameters through guess and check.

- Light Sport Aircraft Automobile: On four-person team, served as lead for numerical analysis and optimization and design analysis assistant. Designed vehicle that would be capable of driving on any road in the U.S. and be able to fly while carrying at least two passengers. Followed commercial vehicle regulations, which constrained aircraft size and the size of control surfaces, which meant folding the wings. Set maximum allowable flight parameters to match that of a light sport aircraft pilot license.

- Automatic Glove Dispenser: Served as CAD design, structural load analysis and design analysis lead for six-person team. Designed and produced alpha prototype of an automatic glove dispenser. Researched, developed, produced and tested various mockups, including materials selection; settled on a top-loading glove dispenser that would utilize gravity to load gloves into a tray, which would allow users to slide their hands into the gloves without touching the outside of the gloves, keeping the gloves sterile.

- ➤ RELEVANT COURSEWORK: Calculus: Multi-variable, Vector and Differential Equations; Statics; Dynamics; Aircraft and Spacecraft Dynamics; Aerodynamics of Aerospace Vehicles; Fluid Mechanics; Compressible Flow; Aerospace Propulsion; Thermodynamics; Applied Thermodynamics (Refrigeration and Heaters); Design of Thermal Systems; Engineering Materials and Design; Analysis of Aerostructures; Systems Analysis and Control; Engineering Measurements; Drafting
Physics: Mechanical, Electrical, and Modern; CAD/CAM with Numerical Control, Spacecraft and Aircraft Mechanics; Design of Mechanical Systems; Heat and Mass Transfer; Finite Element Methods in Engineering; Design of Aerospace Vehicles I (Fixed Wing Aircraft Design Practices); Design of Aerospace Vehicles II (Design of Space Launch Vehicles and Satellites).

WORK EXPERIENCE:

ENGINEERING TECHNICIAN (Intern), GS-0802-05   05/2019-08/2019
United States Coast Guard, Civil Engineering Unit, Honolulu, HI 96850
Hours/week: 40
Supervisor: Neal Kamona, Phone: 808-444-4444, May contact

- APPLIED ENGINEERING PRINCIPLES AND CONCEPT KNOWLEDGE to evaluate designs for $5M C-130 Hercules rinse rack that complied with military regulations and FAA height restrictions. Researched concepts that incorporated a reverse-osmosis water-filtration system to reclaim used water to reduce water usage and that required minimal maintenance over system lifetime. Reviewed plans, manuals, instruction books, technical standards, guides and reports to identify problem areas and assess feasibility. Performed cost analysis on potential rinse rack positions and variety of existing rinse rack systems.

- COMMUNICATED ORALLY AND IN WRITING. Worked closely with engineers, senior and support staff and stakeholders. Coordinated meetings with contracting companies regarding site preparation for C-130 rinse rack at the local air station. Contacted State of Hawai'i officials to obtain as-built drawings for a floating dock project that was slated to moor a pair of 100-foot Coast Guard cutters; coordinated site visits to assess ocean swell conditions at the State of Hawai'i floating dock and assessed the dock's performance.

- USED TECHNICAL SKILLS to update and maintain engineering drawing database by filing as-built, engineering and surveying drawings with proper descriptions of each drawing.

ENGINEERING TECHNICIAN, GS-0802-05   05/2018-09/2018
United States Coast Guard, Base Support Unit, San Pedro, CA 90731
Hours/week: 40
Supervisor: Len Roses, Phone: 310-555-5555, May not contact

- DEMONSTRATED ENGINEERING KNOWLEDGE AND SKILL in consulting with Civil Engineering Unit Oakland (CEU Oakland) and updating drawing database; introduced the office to the system widely used throughout the Coast Guard, replacing the previous method, which used a collection of on hand copies of drawings obtained from CEU Oakland. Developed drawings for base projects, including a living quarters renovation and office space expansion.

ENGINEERING TECHNICIAN, GS-0802-04   06/2017-08/2017
United States Coast Guard- Civil Engineering Unit
Honolulu, HI 96850
Hours/week: 40
Supervisor: Neal Kamona, Phone: 808-555-5555, May contact

- COMMUNICATED ORALLY AND IN WRITING. Performed engineering site visits with design team leader, lead mechanical engineer and lead electrical engineer on installing a new wind turbine system to improve base security when power is cut off and the base needs to be locked down. Went on site visits to improve and maintain jet fuel pumping station holding tanks and pipes used to move the fuel.

- DEMONSTRATED knowledge of professional engineering concepts, principles and practices in engineering development of solar water heating system for Coast Guard locker room under the guidance of the lead mechanical engineer. Performed entire project from design of the system to the system's parts.

- UTILIZED ORGANIZATIONAL SKILLS and knowledge of AutoCAD 2010 to electronically consolidate all current utility drawings of the base into one master drawing that accurately identified the correct position of any utility seen and unseen on the air station.

PROFESSIONAL REFERENCES

Neal Kamona, Design Team Leader, US Coast Guard - Civil Engineering Unit Honolulu
300 Ala Moana Blvd 8-134, Honolulu, HI 96850
Phone Number: 808-888-8888; Email:

Gail Goingo, Lead Architect, US Coast Guard - Civil Engineering Unit Honolulu
300 Ala Moana Blvd 8-134, Honolulu, HI 96850
Phone Number: 808-555-5555; Email:

Marisol Mendez

HIRED!

Presidential Management Fellows
Army National Guard, E-5

Master of Public Policy, Archives and Manuscripts, Study and Writing of History

---

MARISOL MENDEZ
1111 Mystery Lane
Baltimore, MD 21228
Phone: 333-333-3333
Email: Marisol.mendez111@gmail.com

OBJECTIVE: Presidential Management Fellow and/or National Security Policy Internship utilizing Master's in Public Policy and seven years in National Guard experience. Army National Guard, Honorably Discharged, E-5. Veteran's Preference: 10 points for 30 percent or more disability.

EDUCATION

Master's in Public Policy, expected Dec. 2020
Trachtenburg School, George Washington University, Washington, DC
GI Bill and Yellow Ribbon Scholarships

Concentration: National Security Policy. The national security policy field embraces processes of policy-making for national security, the analysis of defense programs, defense economics, the history of warfare and strategy, and the identification and understanding of the national and international security agenda in the 21st century.

Major courses:
ECON 6239: **Economics of National Defense**
HIST 6032: **Seminar on Strategy and Policy**
PSC 6348: **Politics of U.S. National Security Policy**
PSC 6349: **International Security Politics**

MAJOR PAPER: **Seminar on Strategy and Policy: 2002-2004 Analysis and Strategic Plans for the Transition of Guard Readiness and Return to Reserve Status.** Explored the OEF and OIF National Guard Readiness strategies from 2002-2004 to analyze trends and devise recommendations for return to Reserve Status. The thesis and recommendations provide National Guard Readiness policy-makers with a strategic plan for Reserve to Active to Reserve Duty with employment, career and educational planning tools.

2012, Bachelor's Degree, University of Ohio, Dayton, Ohio, Major: Business Administration (27 hours in business courses), GPA, 3.27 out of 4.0.

WORK HISTORY

09/2015 to 08/2018, READINESS NON-COMMISSIONED OFFICER, U.S. Army National Guard, Catonsville, MD; Honorably Discharged

- SENIOR ADVISOR AND ADMINISTERED mobilization readiness program to support unit personnel in preparation for changing deployment requirements.

- MANAGED ANALYTICAL AND EVALUATIVE STUDIES. Oversaw and monitored Military Occupational Specialty qualification program for unit personnel. Planned and coordinated Family Readiness Group activities.

- SUPERVISED AND LED activities of unit support staff and logistics personnel.

- ACCOMPLISHMENTS: Instrumental in preparing 60+ soldiers for deployment in support of Operation Iraqi Freedom. Initiated Family Readiness Group to support over 60 deployed personnel and their dependents; coordinated distribution of care packages to deployed soldiers. Assisted in coordination of deployment of 200 personnel and equipment in support of Operation Enduring Freedom; coordinated pre-deployment convoys to move unit's vehicles to deployment site. Planned and conducted training for 200 personnel.

05/2014 to 09/2015, PROPERTY BOOK NON-COMMISSIONED OFFICER, Maryland National Guard, Reisterstown, MD

- REVIEWED REQUESTS FOR, LOCATED, AND TRANSFERRED required equipment and gear for mobilizing units preparing for deployment, ensuring equipment readiness.

- USED AUTOMATED SYSTEMS, DATABASES AND COMPUTER APPLICATIONS. Prepared and generated unit reports for five battalions within Area Support Group. Verified unit equipment on hand in database, and match to monthly Unit Readiness List.

- ACCOMPLISHMENTS: Located available equipment and prepared documentation for equipment transfers for mobilizing units.

11/2013 to 05/2014, TRAINING NCO/ADMINISTRATOR, Maryland National Guard, 1008 Transportation Company, Reisterstown, MD.

Prepared 40+ unit personnel for deployment in support of Operation Iraqi Freedom. While working at Soldier Readiness Processing site, led team to process hundreds of personnel actions and meet deadlines for required daily processing.

AWARDS, HONORS, RECOGNITION

Global War on Terrorism Service Medal; Army Reserve Component Achievement Medal; National Defense Service Medal; Armed Forces Reserve Medal; Non-Commissioned Officer Professional Development Ribbon 3rd Award; Army Service Ribbon; Armed Forces Reserve Medal with M Device.

Appendix B:
Schedule A Hiring for Persons with Disabilities and Federal Job Numbers

Disability Employment
SELECTIVE PLACEMENT PROGRAM COORDINATOR

Selective Placement Program Coordinator (SPPC) Directory

This directory lists the Selective Placement Program Coordinators in Federal agencies. The headquarters SPPC's can provide information on SPPC's at local installations. OPM updates this directory as needed. Each agency is responsible for monitoring the activities of its designated SPPC's and also for notifying OPM when a new coordinator is selected.

You can filter the following list by choosing a state and/or agency name then clicking the "Filter" button. When searching by state, please keep in mind that each SPPC helps management recruit, hire and accommodate people with disabilities for their agency only, not for all agencies in their state." In addition to an SPPC, many agencies also have a Disability Program Manager who manage and evaluate SPPC's, as well as programs for people with disabilities.

Use the drop down menu to identify search results by agency, state, or use the map below to select a state. States with a green color contain SPPC information.

Search by State:

| Alabama ⌄ | Filter |

OR

Search by Agency:

| All Agencies ⌄ | Filter |

Selective Placement Program Coordinator Directory:
https://www.opm.gov/policy-data-oversight/disability-employment/selective-placement-program-coordinator-directory/

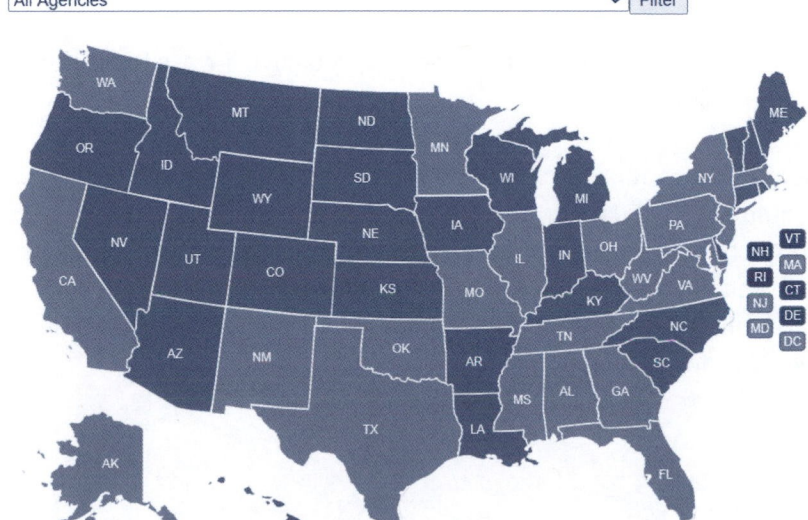

Schedule A Federal Hiring Authority For Students With Disabilities

In Executive Order 12548 of July 26, 2010, President Obama established a hiring increase goal of 100,000 people with disabilities into the federal government over five years, including individuals with targeted disabilities.

My administration is committed to ensuring people living with disabilities have fair access to jobs so they can contribute to our economy and realize their dreams. Individuals with disabilities are a vital and dynamic part of our Nation.
--President Barack Obama, July, 2010

Schedule A is an excepted service hiring authority available to federal agencies to hire and/or promote individuals with disabilities without competing for the job. Schedule A hiring authority allows federal agencies to avoid using the traditional, and sometimes lengthy, competitive hiring process.

Have positions been filled under Schedule A? YES. By the end of Fiscal Year (FY) 2015, total career Federal employment for people with disabilities had increased from 247,608 in FY 2014 to 264,844, representing an increase from 13.56 percent to 14.41 percent. New hires with disabilities increased from 20,618 in FY 2014 to 26,466, representing 19.02 percent, in FY 2015. From FY 2011 to FY 2015, the years Federal agencies have been implementing E.O. 13548; the Federal Government hired 109,575 part-time career and full-time career employees with disabilities. This major milestone exceeded the goal to hire 100,000 people with disabilities. (Source: Report on the Employment of Individuals with Disabilities in the Executive Branch –Sept. 22, 2016) *https://www.opm.gov/policy-data-oversight/diversity-and-inclusion/reports/disability-report-fy2015.pdf*

Application Options for Those With Disabilities

Beyond simply applying without identifying yourself as disabled, you have 3 ways to disclose that you are a person with a disability:

1. Submit your application competitively for a position through USAJOBS (www.usajobs.gov), where approximately 20,000 federal jobs are posted daily. Identify yourself as disabled by checking off that you are authorized to be hired as person with a disability. Be prepared to build your resume if you have not already done so.
2. Directly contact the hiring manager for a position you have identified and send them a copy of your Schedule A Application.

3. Contact the Selective Placement Program Coordinator (SPPC) about particular openings. These hiring officials are on the lookout for talented employees who have disabilities. For a list of the coordinators, go to https://www.opm.gov/policy-data-oversight/disability-employment/selective-placement-program-coordinator-directory/.

4. NEW! Submit your resume to the https://www.wrp.gov/wrp database for students with disabilities. More than 20 federal government agencies regularly utilize the WRP as a recruiting source, with more than 6,500 students obtaining federal employment since 1995.

5. 5. A great reference: The ABCs of Schedule A: https://www.eeoc.gov/abcs-schedule

Why Do I Need a Schedule A Letter?

In order to apply with the disabled status under the special hiring authority, jobseekers must provide proof of a disability, and the Schedule A Letter satisfies that requirement. The Schedule A Letter confirming the disability should be signed by a licensed medical professional, state or private vocational rehabilitation specialist, or any government agency that issues or provides disability benefits. The letter often also notes your job readiness for the work you're seeking. Schedule A Letters are submitted through USAJOBS and are given to other federal hiring authorities. The letter should be brief and to the point, and should not go into details about the nature of your disability. Focus on your skills and experience that will be relevant for that agency's mission and services.

What Does a Schedule A Application Include?

Whether you are applying through USAJOBS or you are sending your application through e-mail to a Selective Placement Officer or hiring manager, the application will be made up of these documents:

1. Your own cover letter
2. Schedule A Letter
3. Federal resume
4. Transcript (if you are applying for positions with your education as a qualification)

Use our easy-to-use free RP Cover Letter Builder to writer your letter: https://resume-place.com/resources/cover-letter-builder/

You can upload the Schedule A Letter, cover letter, and transcripts into USAJOBS along with your resume. Alternatively, you can e-mail these documents separately as attached files to the Selective Placement Program Coordinator (SPPC).

Office of Personnel Management Schedule A Information:
https://www.opm.gov/policy-data-oversight/disability-employment/hiring/#url=Schedule-A-Hiring-Authority

STUDENT'S FEDERAL CAREER GUIDE

Sample Schedule A Letter for Vocational Rehabilitation Professionals

State

| Name of Counselor, M.S., Position Title | *Department of Rehabilitative Services* Street Address – Suite Number City, State Zip Code website | Main Line: xxx-xxx-xxxx TTY: xxx-xxx-xxx Fax: xxx-xxx-xxxx Email: |

Direct Line: xxx-xxx-xxxx

Date

To Whom It May Concern:

This letter serves as certification that (name) is an individual with a documented disability, identified by the (vocational rehabilitation services agency name) policy and can be considered for employment under the Schedule A hiring authority 5 CFR 213.3102 (u) for people with intellectual disabilities, severe physical disabilities or psychiatric disabilities. Thank you for your interest in considering this individual for employment. You may contact me at (contact information).

Sincerely,

(Vocational rehabilitation professional's signature)

Sample Schedule A Letter for Licensed Medical Practitioners

The letter must be printed on "medical professional's" letterhead and must include a signature or it is invalid.

Date

To Whom It May Concern:

This letter serves as certification that (name of patient/applicant) is an individual with an intellectual disability, severe physical disability or psychiatric disability, and can be considered for employment under the Schedule A hiring authority 5 CFR 213,3102(u). Thank you for your interest in considering this individual for employment. You may contact me at (phone number).

Sincerely,

(Medical professional's signature)

(Medical professional's title)

Top 30 Job Titles in the Federal Government

Only jobs with an asterisk (*) require a degree or specific education.

Job Title (Series Number)	No. of U.S. employees
0301-MISCELLANEOUS ADMINISTRATION AND PROGRAM	104,942
0610-NURSE	86,400
2210-INFORMATION TECHNOLOGY MANAGEMENT	84,097
0343-MANAGEMENT AND PROGRAM ANALYSIS	74,361
0303-MISCELLANEOUS CLERK AND ASSISTANT	54,026
1802-COMPLIANCE INSPECTION AND SUPPORT	51,890
1811-CRIMINAL INVESTIGATION	43,160
0905-GENERAL ATTORNEY	38,472
1801-GENERAL INSPECTION, INVESTIGATION, ENFORCEMENT, AND COMPLIANCE SERIES	38,175
1102-CONTRACTING	37,752
0602-MEDICAL OFFICER	35,195
0679-MEDICAL SUPPORT ASSISTANCE	30,121
0962-CONTACT REPRESENTATIVE	30,108
0201-HUMAN RESOURCES MANAGEMENT	29,830
0105-SOCIAL INSURANCE ADMINISTRATION	27,538
0801-GENERAL ENGINEERING	26,780
1101-GENERAL BUSINESS AND INDUSTRY	26,675
0501-FINANCIAL ADMINISTRATION AND PROGRAM	25,773
1895-CUSTOMS AND BORDER PROTECTION	22,961
0401-GENERAL NATURAL RESOURCES MANAGEMENT AND BIOLOGICAL SCIENCES	21,130
2152-AIR TRAFFIC CONTROL	20,546
0346-LOGISTICS MANAGEMENT	20,315
1896-BORDER PATROL ENFORCEMENT SERIES	19,261
0620-PRACTICAL NURSE	19,194
0855-ELECTRONICS ENGINEERING	18,556
0007-CORRECTIONAL OFFICER	17,734
0185-SOCIAL WORK	16,995
0340-PROGRAM MANAGEMENT	15,718
0601-GENERAL HEALTH SCIENCE	15,517
0621-NURSING ASSISTANT	14,712
0083-POLICE	14,690

*Original Research, Resume Place, Inc., Dec. 2019.
https://www.fedscope.opm.gov/employment.asp

STUDENT'S **FEDERAL CAREER GUIDE**

Top Agency Hires

Agency	Oct–Dec 2016	Jan–Mar 2017	Apr–Jun 2017	Jul–Sep 2017	FY 2017
Agency - All	47408	40690	56361	44905	189364
CABINET LEVEL AGENCIES	**45289**	**38093**	**54858**	**40357**	**178597**
Department of Veterans Affairs	9585	8611	9755	12355	40306
Department of Homeland Security	5994	4485	4370	6342	21191
Department of the Army	5450	3154	5703	5074	19381
Department of Agriculture	2027	2461	12033	1295	17816
Department of the Interior	1599	2104	7125	1238	12066
Department of the Air Force	3763	2261	3087	2672	11783
Department of the Navy	2874	1846	3206	3518	11444
Department of Defense	3233	1766	2190	2925	10114
LARGE INDEPENDENT AGENCIES (1000 OR MORE EMPLOYEES)	**1798**	**2137**	**1219**	**4290**	**9444**
Department of the Treasury	3123	4316	688	160	8287
Department of Justice	1822	1729	1746	1461	6758
Department of Health and Human Services	2256	1743	1366	1299	6664
Department of Commerce	1593	1660	2295	946	6494
Department of Transportation	1018	1001	930	748	3697
Social Security Administration	104	51	371	1840	2366
Small Business Administration	308	99	24	1564	1995
MEDIUM INDEPENDENT AGENCIES (100-999 EMPLOYEES)	**278**	**378**	**233**	**208**	**1097**
National Aeronautics and Space Administration	130	470	66	171	837
Environmental Protection Agency	253	433	75	38	799
Department of Energy	207	242	212	109	770
Department of State	283	225	68	79	655
General Services Administration	254	189	127	77	647
Department of Labor	226	281	23	40	570
Office of Personnel Management	107	147	68	133	455
Department of Housing and Urban Development	137	123	35	78	373
Federal Deposit Insurance Corporation	22	50	170	109	351
Smithsonian Institution	119	125	42	63	349
Department of Education	99	85	26	18	228
SMALL INDEPENDENT AGENCIES (LESS THAN 100 EMPLOYEES)	**43**	**82**	**51**	**50**	**226**
National Science Foundation	71	57	38	46	212
National Archives and Records Administration	62	69	7	65	203
Peace Corps	74	63	27	20	184
Federal Reserve System	23	75	59	15	172
Securities and Exchange Commission	79	49	12	11	151
Agency for International Development	42	58	16	27	143
Federal Trade Commission	19	29	56	30	134
Office of Management And Budget	28	45	26	31	130
Corporation for National and Community Service	30	54	8	17	109
Equal Employment Opportunity Commission	38	51	0	3	92
Federal Housing Finance Agency	9	8	48	10	75
Consumer Product Safety Commission	18	9	44	1	72
National Labor Relations Board	17	31	4	13	65
Broadcasting Board of Governors	14	35	3	11.	63
Federal Communications Commission	17	17	7	20	61
Government Printing Office	13	13	22	11	59
Pension Benefit Guaranty Corporation	22	31	0	3	56
National Foundation on the Arts and the Humanities	16	20	4	15	55

*Original Research, Resume Place, Inc., Dec. 2019.

https://www.fedscope.opm.gov/employment.asp

PUBLICATIONS BY THE RESUME PLACE, INC.

Order online at www.resume-place.com | Bulk Orders: (888) 480 8265
BULK PRICES for Bulk Book purchases for Federal agencies
E-books available for immediate download at www.resume-place.com

Ten Steps to a Federal Job® or Internship for Recent Grads and Students, 4th Edition.
Third edition won the 2013 IndieFab Gold Winner for Career Books! Outstanding book for jobseekers who are just getting out of college and whose education will help the applicant get qualified for a position. Numerous samples of recent graduate resumes with emphasis on college degrees, courses, major papers, internships, and relevant work experiences. *$15.95. Print book or eBook.*

Federal Resume Guidebook, 7th Edition – All New Jan 2020—Now the #2 resume book in America! The ultimate Federal resume writing and career change guide for government careers! *$15.95. $10 ea for 50+ books + shipping.*

The Stars Are Lined Up for Military Spouses, 2nd Edition—Key book to assist military spouses with navigating USAJOBS and the complex Federal job process. Covers four ways to land the major kinds of federal positions for military spouses. *$14.95. $8 ea for 50+ books + shipping.*

Jobseeker's Guide, 8th Edition—Military to Federal Career Transition Resource. Workbook and guide for the Ten Steps to a Federal Job® training curriculum. Federal job search strategies for first-time jobseekers who are separating military and family members. *$18.95. $8 ea for 50+ books + shipping.*

The New SES Application, 2nd Edition, breaks down this complex application process into a step-by-step guide based on a popular workshop taught for over 10 years. Updated with Senior Executive Service info to help you navigate hiring reforms currently impacting the SES. *$21.95. Bulk rates available.*

Creating Your First Resume is a book used at high school and technical school programs nationwide. The new edition boasts brand new resume samples that represent the push toward STEM technical programs. Useful for providing training and certifications for high school students. *$12.95. $5 ea for 50+ books + shipping.*

Federal Resume Database—This online resource contains more than 110 resume samples and Federal job search resources from the current Resume Place publications. Sample resumes are available in Word & PDF format for easy reading and editing. *Individual and Agency / Base Licenses available.*

RESUME PLACE

BUILDING CAREERS IN THE US GOVERNMENT

About the Author:
Kathryn Troutman

1. Founder, President, and Manager of The Resume Place®, the first Federal job search consulting and Federal resume writing service in the world, and the producer of www.resume-place.com, the first website devoted to Federal resume writing.

2. Pioneer designer of the Federal resume format in 1995 with the publication of the leading resource for Federal human resources and jobseekers worldwide—the *Federal Resume Guidebook*—now in its sixth edition and the #2 resume book on the internet.

3. Developer of the Certified Federal job Search Trainer®/Certified Federal Career Coach® train-the-trainer program in 2002. Licensing *Ten Steps to a Federal Job®*, a curriculum and turnkey training program taught by more than 5,000 Certified Federal Job Search Trainers® (CFJST) around the world. Recommended by military services for transition and employment readiness counselors around the world.

FEDERAL CAREER CERTIFICATION AND LICENSING

Certified Federal Job Search Trainer / Certified Federal Career Coach - CFJST / CFCC

Three formats available: 3-day in-person training; 7-part, 90 minute webinars; or hosted class at your location.

Learn now to teach government civilians, service members, military spouses, students, veterans, first-time Federal jobseekers about the successful step--by-step approach to Federal job search and Federal resume writing.

Get licensed to teach the following curriculum for 3 years:

1. Ten Steps to a Federal Job®
2. The Stars are Lined Up for Military Spouses®
3. Creating Your First Resume
4. Ten Steps to a Federal Job® or Internship for Students and Recent Graduates

More info, dates, rates and registration: *www.resume-place.com*

FEDERAL RESUME WRITING – JOBSEEKER SERVICES - CONSULTING, WRITING, EDITING

RP Certified Federal Resume Writers and Coaches for Jobseekers